Writing To Sell

To Alexandra,
for more than words can say

Writing To Sell

*The Complete Guide to
Copywriting for Business*

Kit Sadgrove

ROBERT HALE · LONDON

ISBN 0 7090 4676 6

Robert Hale Limited
Clerkenwell House
Clerkenwell Green
London EC1R 0HT

Set in Sabon by
Derek Doyle & Associates, Mold, Clwyd.
Printed in Great Britain by
St Edmundsbury Press, Bury St Edmunds, Suffolk.
Bound by WBC Bookbinders Ltd, Bridgend, Glamorgan.

Contents

Preface

Have you ever felt envious of professionally written advertising copy? Have you ever felt you could write the words – if only you knew where to start? *Writing to Sell* solves that problem. It provides clear and simple advice on how to write for business.

All kinds of people will find this book useful. Even major advertisers need to write their own material occasionally. Some copy is too urgent or too small to hand to an agency; and big advertising agencies are notoriously unable to handle simple brochures.

Smaller advertisers may be forced by lack of budget to write their own copy. And there are some jobs where detailed product knowledge makes you the best person to write the words. Giving this type of job to an agency will entail laborious briefings, followed by numerous changes to the text.

Companies often draft words for an advertising agency, only to have the copy returned with few alterations but a big invoice. Now you can feel confident enough to write polished final copy.

Even if you employ an agency, you must be able to evaluate its work. How do you decide whether the copy is right? *Writing to Sell* shows you how to be a skilled judge – more skilled perhaps than even the agency's copywriters.

Unlike other books on the subject, *Writing to Sell* doesn't concentrate on one particular marketing tool, such as advertising. It covers *all* the main methods of communication. That is because most businesses make good use of all the options available to them, including PR, sales literature and direct mail. These are the topics that business people themselves tend to write, and these are the ones where more help is needed. This wider approach makes *Writing to Sell* a useful book for everyone involved in marketing.

1 *Writing to Sell*

It's time to throw away your copies of Charles Dickens, time to forget the English lessons you learnt at school. The language of advertising is different from the schoolroom.

The people who read your words are busy. They aren't interested in your product. They're interested in themselves. So it's vital to communicate well.

Readers need to know what benefits your product will give them. They will be impressed by clear words, simple explanations and a logical flow – not by flowery words or slow sentences.

The first task is to identify your customers. Even if you know them well, it is worth considering their mood and location when they see your communication. Doing this will sharpen your writing. Below are some questions to ask yourself.

READER CHECK LIST

Whom are you writing for?
How much do they know about your company, and your product?
How interested are they in your product?
How educated are they?
What do they want to know?
Why are they reading the publication?
What degree of detail do they need, and in what stages?
What fears or worries do they have?
What are the benefits you are offering?
Why would they buy your products rather than your competitors?

What is your customers' frame of mind when they read your message?
Where will they read your message (in the office, at home, on the train)?

Analysing the reader: what sort of person is he?
Having got a clear picture of your reader, you should assess the sort of writing that is needed. From a postcard to a 36-page brochure, from selling pencils to computers, every type of writing is different.

WRITING CHECK LIST

What is the most important point to convey?
What other points do you want to cover?
In what form will the writing appear (direct mail, leaflet, window display)?
How much detail do you need to provide?
Where does this writing fit in the overall selling process? Is it the first communication? Or is it in response to an advertisement?
Do you have all the background information you need?
What should your writing achieve? Should it change opinions or make a sale?
How does the writing take the reader to the next stage? Is there a coupon or a sales hotline?

Use this checklist to decide the style and content of your writing.

GETTING STARTED

There is nothing worse than facing a blank sheet of paper without knowing where to start. Some people can write like Shakespeare; the rest of us have to sweat over it. Here are some tips for getting started.

- Put down all the points that occur to you. Don't worry about their relative order or importance – just get them on to paper.
- Start with an easy section. Break the work into manageable chunks. By the inch it's a cinch.

- List your thoughts as bullet points (like this text). Don't worry about writing proper sentences.
- Jot down thoughts for headlines. Don't stop at one – write as many as you can think of.
- Leave grammar, spelling and sentence construction until last. Don't waste half an hour trying to improve one sentence. If you leave it alone, it will come to you in time.
- By now the text should be in roughly the right order. Start replacing the bullet points with proper sentences. Make sure the most important points are at the beginning of the text.
- Read the work aloud, listening for passages that don't sound right. Rephrase any sentences that sound clumsy.
- Show the work to someone else, and be prepared to accept their criticisms.
- Finally, proof-read the work to get rid of errors. Read out every word slowly, putting a ruler underneath each line.

TEN WAYS OF AVOIDING WRITER'S BLOCK

1   Try a change of scene. Go for a walk, make a cup of coffee, or work on a different project for a while.
2   Relax. Thoughts often come when you aren't concentrating too hard. Think about the task when you're in the bath or out driving. Carry a pocket recorder in the car and have a notepad by the bath.
3   Focus on a specific customer. What would he want to know? How would you talk to him?
4   Go where you can avoid interruptions. Find a room that has pleasant but business-like surroundings.
5   Don't work on the problem in ten-minute snatches, unless this suits your way of working. Most people need an uninterrupted hour or two to get into writing.
6   Set a deadline. The best work is produced against a time limit.
7   Work when you are at your best. Decide whether you perform better in the morning or at night.
8   If you're still stuck, tell a colleague or your spouse about the work. Tell them what you are trying to convey. Discussing the problem will help to clarify it in your mind.

9   Still stuck? Design the structure of the piece. Write down
    the main headings.
10 If all else fails, open a bottle of wine.

HOW MUCH SHOULD YOU WRITE?

Let's say you're writing a full-page advertisement. Find an ad
with a layout similar to yours and count its words. Then find
an ad that looks too crowded, and count the words. This will
give you a range to work within, perhaps 100 to 200 words.

There are surprisingly few words in advertisements and
brochures, and this is an important point. If you write too
many words, you clog the page and discourage readers.

THE RIGHT SENTENCE LENGTH

The sentence length depends on the medium you are using
(whether a press ad or a sales leaflet). Ten words per sentence
is about right for press advertisements, while fifteen-word
sentences suit direct mail and brochures. Any sentence that
exceeds twenty-five words will be too difficult to follow.

It is easy to write in a rambling way, to keep adding points
as they occur to you. Cut the sentences into manageable
lengths by isolating the different points. Vary short sentences
with long ones, to prevent the text from becoming tedious.

Short sentences often work well. If used sparingly, they
spice up the text and stop it from being boring. They can add
a sense of urgency.

But they aren't right for every situation. Sometimes they
seem too brash. If you're selling country kitchens or an
accountancy service, short sentences would give the wrong
impression. They can look jerky, especially if they lack a
main verb. Like this sentence.

Short sentences are more suited to advertisements, where
the entire copy can be read in twenty seconds. But brochures,
like books, need longer sentences because the reader needs to
settle down for a good read.

YOU'VE GOT TO HAVE RHYTHM

Every piece of writing should have a rhythm. It isn't the
rhythm of poetry, but it swirls like water in a stream. All the
water goes in the same general direction and at roughly the
same speed, but there are enough eddies to provide an

ever-changing pattern.

Read your work aloud when you have finished it. If you get to a part that you stumble over, try rewriting it. You could shorten it, express it more simply, get rid of figures of speech, or chop it into two sentences.

ACHIEVING THE RIGHT PARAGRAPH LENGTH

A paragraph of more than fifteen lines is off-putting. A hundred years ago, people had greater powers of concentration. But thirty-second TV commercials and ten-second sound bites have reduced their attention span.

Check your text. If it resembles a forest of words, divide it into smaller pieces. Split the paragraph after several sentences.

A press advertisement can have paragraphs containing just one sentence. That is fine when the pace is fast, when there are many ideas to convey, and when each paragraph contains a single idea. But one-sentence paragraphs look too hasty in the measured text found in leaflets or press releases.

THE CLARITY CHART

You can judge the clarity of your work by checking it against the Clarity Chart.

Count the total number of words in your text. Divide it by the number of sentences. This gives you the average number of words per sentence (column 1).

Then count the number of syllables in the first 100 words (column 2). Draw a straight line linking the two points, and see where the line reaches column 3.

1 Average number of words per sentence	2 Number of syllables per 100 words	3 Readability
1-3	100-150	Very easy
4-10	151-190	Easy
11-16	190-200	Moderate
17-25	200-215	Moderate
26-35	215-230	Difficult
36+	231-250	Very difficult

The Clarity Chart makes a simple point. The longer the sentences, and the longer the words, the more difficult it is to read the text.

EMPLOY STRONG HEADLINES

A headline should always encourage people to read the text. It should make them curious, or make them think they will learn something to their advantage. Be bold when it comes to headlines: they are the secret of getting people to read your words. Use long headlines freely: they work as well as short ones.

Never make the headline obscure. Never use words that people won't understand, as in this charity headline:

> More women are victims of intestacy than divorce.

Even ordinary brochures need stimulating headlines. Brochures often waste an opportunity by using dull headlines like 'Introduction', or 'Product Characteristics'.

USE CROSSHEADS

Crossheads are the minor headings that break up groups of paragraphs in newspapers. Their role is to attract the eye to the text and make it easier to read. Newspapers have the advantage of being able to add words like 'Crisis' or 'Sex'. You're unlikely to be able to use words like this. But you can still select the most evocative word from a group of paragraphs.

Use at least two headlines or subheads per page of text. They will guide the reader through the page.

BANISH ABSTRACT WORDS

Avoid using abstract words, like 'adjustment'. If you find you have written one, change it into a verb or use a concrete noun.

People like using abstract words because they sound weighty. They help the writer feel grand, but they also reduce the reader's understanding.

In the following ad from a telemarketing company, the abstract words have been underlined to show just how many there are.

A telephone marketing campaign takes experience and intelligent planning. It means co-ordinating the message, the execution, the fulfilment and the analysis.

And it requires a telephone marketing service with the technological and human resources to make every call count … With expert account handling from initial consultation to smooth implementation.

Abstract words usually have an extra syllable, an extra few letters to confuse the reader. Put in too many abstract ideas and the reader will begin to founder.

TURNING ABSTRACT WORDS INTO THEIR CONCRETE EQUIVALENTS

Avoid this abstract noun:	**by using a more easily understood word like:**
Cessation	Stop
Confidentiality	Secret
Directorship	Director
Documentation	Forms
Employment	Work
Evaluation	Decide, judge
Exclusiveness	Exclusive
Implementation	Do
Indication	Sign
Installation	Do
Management	Managers
Methodology	Method
Motivation	Keen
Objectivity	Clear
Performance	Perform
Productivity	Output
Proximity	Close
Regulation	Regulate
Remuneration	Pay
Synthesis	Join
Transportation	Lorries
Understanding	Know

Abstract nouns can be translated into verbs, concrete nouns or even adjectives.

WORDS THAT LACK MEANING
Here is a set of words that are so general as to lack meaning. Many have been worn out by overuse. Try to use a more concrete word in their place.

Administration
Authority
Characteristic
Commitment
Consideration
Context
Facility
Information
Intrinsic
Involvement
Operational
Policy
Procedure
Relationship
Situation
Standards
Strategy
Structure
System

DON'T USE LONG WORDS
Long words are more difficult to read, and fewer people understand their meaning. Even PhDs find it easier to read 'above' than 'superjacent'. And 'big' means the same as 'considerable'. True, you lost subtle shades of meaning when you only use small words. But think of the rewards: more readers, more understanding, more interest and more sales.

Go through your work, hunting for words with more than three syllables. When you find them, substitute a shorter word. Here are some long business words that should be exchanged for something shorter. You may have to change the sentence around to achieve this. You may even have to use several smaller words.

EXCHANGING LONG WORDS FOR SHORT ONES

When you want to use this word:	Try this one instead:
Achievement	Success
Advantageous	Good, cheap
Application	Effort, job
Appreciation	Thanks
Appropriate	Right
Communicate	Tell
Component	Part
Concerning	About
Consequence	Result
Considerable	Large
Consultation	Discuss
Development	Develop, begin
Diagnosis	Decide
Discover	Find
Dysfunctional	Not working
Fundamental	Major
Inventory	Stock
Magnitude	Large
Memoranda	Memos
Organization	Firm
Organizational	This word is often irrelevant
Participative	Sharing
Purchase	Buy
Schedule	Plan
Select	Choose
Subsequent	Future
Symptomatic	Example
Technological	Advanced
Unsatisfactory	Poor
Utilization	Use

Some words refuse to be shortened. The words 'Certification body' convey a lot of meaning about a certain type of organization and its role. But take the word 'environment'. Sometimes it is used in its strictly ecological sense. At other times it is superfluous. 'The worsening economic environment' really means 'the worsening economy'.

'Specification' sometimes means plans and documents for a particular contract, and this cannot easily be shortened; at other times it simply means the job itself.

Some words become common inside a company. For example 'Internalization' and 'Mechanization' are shorthand for quite complex processes. It is acceptable to use these words in internal memos, but you should avoid them in messages to outside audiences.

Long-winded words are sometimes the sign of an older person or an old-fashioned outlook. If you need to prove that your product works efficiently, has modern design and is speedily delivered, keep the words short.

YOU: THE MOST POWERFUL WORD IN ADVERTISING

Don't be afraid to use the word 'you'. No piece of writing needs to be unfriendly or pompous. Think of the least friendly piece of writing: it would probably be a legal contract. Here is a real piece of legal jargon from an order form:

> The Customer is strictly liable for any loss or damage to the magnetic tapes however caused while they are in the Customer's possession.

How much clearer it would be to read:

> You are strictly liable for any loss or damage to the magnetic tapes, however caused, while they are in your possession.

Your solicitor will tell you it is essential to phrase the words in his style. If you seriously applied this reasoning, every advertisement would look like a legal document. Banish all legal jargon wherever you meet it.

IDIOMS REDUCE UNDERSTANDING

Avoid using idioms unless you have to. They force the reader to translate what you are saying, and that complicates life unnecessarily. Nearly every idiom has a simpler alternative. Here are a few.

A law unto himself	Strong willed
At a snail's pace	Slow
At your wits' end	In despair
Be thick-skinned	Insensitive
Cater for	Serve
Close to my heart	Important
Cost a pretty penny	Be expensive
Cost an arm and a leg	Be expensive
Fed up to the teeth with	Irritated by
Get cold feet	Be anxious
Get into your head	Believe
Give someone a free hand	Delegate
Give the game away	Reveal
Have no stomach for	Not want
Have one's work cut out	Be busy
Know it like the palm of my hand	Know it well
Make your way in the world	Succeed
Money down the drain	Wasteful
Pay through the nose	Pay a lot
Play an important role	Be important
Price ourselves out of the market	Too expensive
Pull the rug from under his feet	Forestall
Pushed for time	Busy
Stand in the way	Prevent
Stay on the right side of the law	Be honest
Stick to your guns	Stay firm
Take the wind out of his sails	Forestall
Take your life in your hands	Act decisively
Wild goose chase	Useless trip

Many of these are euphemisms – a way of talking around the subject without actually saying the words. They use four words where one will do.

USING ABBREVIATIONS

Words like 'couldn't' or 'won't' can be used in chatty copy. They can be used in most advertisements, but take care in using them in more formal copy.

If in doubt, ask yourself whether the unabbreviated words look too stiff, or whether (by contrast) the short form looks a little vulgar. See what professional copywriters have done in a similar context.

WEASEL WORDS

When you say that your company is 'one of the biggest', or that your customers are 'almost certain to enjoy' your product, you're using weasel words. They protect the writer from over-claiming, but they are also seen by the consumer for what they are – the cheating words of a company that doesn't feel confident about the claims it makes. Here are some more weasel words:

- Design is arguably one of the most important functions.
- It could be a good investment.
- This could help you lose weight.

Try to make your claims open and candid. Don't say, as a cleaning company did: 'Our service will most likely save you money' – take out those weasel words.

What is the worst that can happen? You might have to reset an advertisement or reprint a leaflet. Unless your claim is really outrageous, people are unlikely to complain.

CHOOSING THE RIGHT WORD

With more people trusting their spellcheck to get the words right, a new type of error is creeping into promotional material. These are the words that in another context would be spelt correctly, but which are wrong in this one. One company claimed that:

> Dry carpet cleaning is not knew, it has been around for about fifty years.

Watch out for the difference between confusing pairs of words. Try replacing your word with the one in brackets to see which fits better.

Advise (to suggest)	Advice (a suggestion)
Affect (to change)	Effect (a result)
Among (among several)	Between (between two)
Compliment (flatter)	Complement (complete)
Council (a gathering)	Counsel (information)
Ensure (make sure)	Insure (protect against)

Fewer (of many)	Less (of one thing)
Illusion (fake)	Allusion (reference)
Its (belonging to)	It's (it is)
Imply (indicate)	Infer (assume)
License (to permit)	Licence (a permit)
Loose (not tight)	Lose (misplace)
Mail (post)	Male (man)
Our (belonging to us)	Are ('the machines are new')
Principal (the first)	Principle (a matter of honour)
Precede (go before)	Proceed (move)
Rite (a ritual)	Right (a direction, a freedom)
Seam (a line)	Seem (appear)
Sight (vision)	Site (location)
Stationary (motionless)	Stationery (writing material)
Tail (ending)	Tale (story)
There (like 'here')	Their (belonging to them)
They're (they are)	Their (belonging to them)
Through (across)	Though (despite)
Too (also)	Two (2); to (towards)
Weather (climate)	Whether (if)
Write (mark)	Right (correct)

NEW WORDS

New words are always being added to the language. We 'bankroll' a company or 'chair' a meeting, and young musicians now 'début'. Avoid new words if they look out of place in your writing, but use them if they save several words.

JOINED WORDS

Words are increasingly being joined together to become one word. There is no reason why words shouldn't be joined, but it rarely improves legibility. If in doubt, keep them apart.

WRITING ABOUT THE COMPANY

A company is a singular noun. So one would normally say:

JTL has won a major contract.

However, many people talk about a company in the plural. The confusion occurs when people talk about the company as 'we'. This is implied in:

Baltic wish to congratulate R.J. Dudmore on its twenty-fifth anniversary.

The situation is further complicated when the company's name ends in 's', such as 'Johnsons', making it look like a plural entity. Taken from a newsletter, the following text slides from singular to plural, and back again:

A.W. Mendips maintain their excellent up-to-date service ... the company maintain ... the company still owns the freehold ... Mendips has retained the personal touch ... A.W. Mendips is not a company to rest on its laurels ... A.W. Mendips are determined ...

It is worth laying down some rules about the use of singulars and plurals:

1 'The company' is always singular.
2 Company names like 'J. Bloggs' should be singular if possible. This means one would say, 'J. Bloggs plans to exhibit ... ' (but see point 4).
3 It is correct to use the plural when talking about 'we'. So you can say, 'We at J. Bloggs are proud of the company's progress. It is a well-established firm.' You can continue, 'Our shower heads produce a fine spray'. This is a little more friendly than 'Its shower heads produce a fine spray.'
4 If the company name looks like a plural (for example, 'Simons'), you might decide to keep it plural throughout. However, this rarely looks so elegant.
5 Try to avoid switching between singular and plural in the same piece of text, to avoid confusing your reader.

SPLITTING THE INFINITIVE
Scholars say you shouldn't split an infinitive. It means you can't write:

To simply present the facts about civil engineering is not enough. It is vital to thoroughly analyse them.

Many people are convinced that split infinitives are wrong.

Very few actually know what is wrong with them. If you are writing for an old or highly educated audience, avoid splitting an infinitive – they will delight in complaining. For other audiences, split your infinitives in the confidence that they won't notice. It sounds odd and the sense is obscured if you write:

> Boldly to go where no man has gone before.

CAPITALS

Use capital letters only when you are referring to the names of people, products and places and things. For example, 'In Ribchester, Mel Morrow presented a seminar on the use of Metropolis gantries.'

Use capitals for people's titles (Mr Jones, Managing Director of GNA Products), but lower case if the title doesn't refer to anyone in particular ('every managing director has new legal responsibilities').

Never say 'It has been a successful year for the Firm'; this is solicitor's English. Just because the word is important to you is not enough to justify a capital letter. See how a newspaper or magazine treats capitals, and adopt that formula.

HOW TO LINK SENTENCES

Sentences benefit from linking words. They help the reader see how the argument flows. Some words let you add more information:

Also
Even more importantly,
For
In addition to
In fact
Including
Indeed
Likewise
Look at
Moreover,
Not only that, but
Not to mention

Plus,
Similarly,
That includes
The really good news, though, is that
Then
What's more

Other words allow you to explain, or take the argument a
stage further:

Actually
As a result
Because
Consequently
For example
Hence
Provided that
Take (the M109 for example)
That's why
Which means that
You see,

Some words let you look at the subject from a different point
of view:

Above all
Although
At the same time
But
But what about
Consider
Conversely
Despite
For our part
However
In comparison
In contrast
Look at it this way
Mind you
On the contrary

On the other hand
Nevertheless
Some people think
Still
The result is
Unfortunately
When you think
Yet

Other words let you move to another, unconnected idea:

Again
Of course
Remember
Since
Whatever your need
While
You'll find

There are powerful introductory words:

For just one week
How many times have you wanted …
It's the only
It's your biggest nightmare
New
Now
Only
Sale

There are words that make it sound easy:

All you have to do
Just flick a switch
Naturally
One simple answer
Quite simply
The most common problem
What more could you ask for?

You can entice your reader:

Discover how
Imagine
Take advantage of
You'll also benefit from

You can share experiences:

Have you ever
It's happened to me
Like us,
Most people
Not everyone
Sometimes
Some of us
You probably

Or you can look ahead:

We'll send you
You'll now be able

You can put the arguments in order:

First, second, next, and finally
From ... to
Meanwhile
Next
Then
Thereafter
To begin with
While

Add detail:

For example
For instance
Further
Furthermore

Specifically

Make a comparison:

A few ... many ...
At home ... abroad ...
At home ... at work ...
Consider ... analyse ...
Not everyone ... but all of us ...
Some ... others ...
Today ... tomorrow ...

Or give reassurance:

All orders are despatched by the next post
Our money-back offer ...
Thousands of people have already ...
We're the biggest name in
You can't lose

You can wrap up the argument, or restate it:

All in all
Briefly
Finally
In conclusion
In other words
In short
In summary
Simply stated
So
Therefore
Thus

At the end of the copy, call for action

For a demonstration
For further information
For immediate details
Post the coupon today

Ring, or write for
To book
To find out more

WRITE COMPLETE SENTENCES
Except for TV commercials and the snappiest of press ads,
you should aim to write complete sentences. It may sound
old-fashioned, but writing proper English aids understanding. The following sentence appeared in a 114-page colour
brochure.

> Then your ferry departure dates and route if possible.

The sentence is missing the verb 'select', which had appeared
in the previous sentence. If you are instructing people in
complex tasks, make your instructions clear. Even when the
text is simple, don't complicate it by omitting main verbs
unless you are writing very short advertising copy.

TIPS TO MAKE YOUR WORK MORE PUNCHY
1   Don't start a sentence with the company name
Avoid starting a sentence with the product or company name.
It puts the reader off, because it looks like a hard sell.

2   Start with a subordinate clause
Try starting some of your sentences with a subordinate
clause. These begin with words like 'When' or 'since', and
they ease the reader into the sentence. Here are a few
examples:

- Considering how important ...
- If you are looking for ...
- Made from the finest leather, the new ...
- When the specification calls for ...
- When you think how much ...
- While not everyone can afford ...

3   Avoid jargon
The trouble with jargon is that not everyone understands it.
Many customers won't know as much about your product as
you do. Some will be new to the market. Others will use a

different word for the same machine. Even old-timers would confess to ignorance if only they dared. If the customer doesn't understand what it means, he can't buy your product. So avoid using jargon, or explain what it means.

Jargon is commonly found in high-tech subjects like computers and biotechnology. But it also occurs in more simple markets. Can you guess what this jargon refers to:

Crab's claw, smooth wall, neck orifice, jetting aperture, self-clearing pin, wadless, dispensing closure.

All these words relate to the humble bottle cap, proving that even the simplest industry has its own strange words.

If you have to use jargon, explain what it means the first time you use it. It is simple to follow the word by a brief explanation in brackets. For example:

The nacelle (or cabin) houses the gears, generator and brake.

If necessary, list each of the words in a box and explain what they mean.

4   Don't use words that are really pauses
Don't use introductory words that add little to the sentence. 'We are pleased to announce the opening of ... ' really means 'We have opened'. Some words can be completely cut without affecting the sense:

Actually
Another consideration that should be taken into account is
A significant factor
At this point in time
In fact
In respect of
In terms of
It is worth noting that
Let us first consider
Of course
Persuant to
Regarding
The main problem to arise was that whilst

Undoubtedly
With respect to

Other words slow down the sentence. Here are some examples of literary throat clearing, with a suggested alternative in brackets:

Bring to a conclusion (end)
End result (result)
Exhibit a tendency (tend)
For a period (for)
Last but not least (finally)
In close proximity (close)
In connection with (about)
In the foreseeable future (in the future)
Involves the use of (uses)
More often than not (often)
Subsequent to (after)

5   Beware of clichés
All awards are 'coveted'. All contracts are 'prestigious'. And every large company is a 'market leader'. People use these clichés because they want to seem enthusiastic about the company. But as the same words are used all the time, they quickly lose their power. Here are more clichéd pairs to avoid.

Complete package
Enviable reputation
Extensive range
Major impact
Professional service
Significant development
Unique product

6   Don't tack prepositions to verbs
Check your work for unnecessary bits stuck on to verbs. Here are a few of the more common ones:

Fit in with

Match up to
Separate out
Split up into
Stick on to

7 Don't use slang

It ain't a good idea to use hip words 'cos they get out of date
so quick you never know whether they sound naff or wicked.
Avoid slang unless you are selling jeans or some other
product that needs street credibility.

SEXIST LANGUAGE

English is changing as society recognizes a wider role for
women. 'Fireman' is changing to 'fire fighter', and
'policeman' to 'police-officer'.

With many females now in executive positions, it looks
increasingly old-fashioned to talk about 'businessmen'. It is
better to use 'business people', or 'people in business', or
'executives' or 'the customer'.

Other words are proving less easy to shift. 'Chairman' has
stuck, in preference to 'Chairperson'. 'The Chair' is now a
possible choice, being no more strange than a collection of
people calling themselves a Board.

There is also a problem when referring to someone as 'he',
when it might also refer to 'she'. For example:

Your baby has special needs. He depends on you for
everything.

It is unacceptable here to say 'she/he', and it sounds legalistic
to say 'him or her'. You could use 'him' and add a footnote
indicating that the text applies to both males and females.
This sounds rather earnest. A better solution would be to
vary the use of 'him' and 'her' to show that the product is
relevant to both. In some cases, you can avoid the problem
completely by talking about 'your baby/spouse/gerbil'.

VERBS ARE BEST

Make good use of verbs, the 'doing' words. These are the
strongest of all the words. Say, 'We sell bathroom suites'
rather than 'Our sales are in bathroom suites'. Write, 'ABC

Bureau hires quality staff' rather than 'ABC organizes the employment of quality staff'.

Always use the verb to convey the sense. Say, 'We will consider any application,' rather than 'We will give consideration to any application'.

USE ACTIVE VERBS

It is easy to use passive verbs without noticing. They can be spotted by their use of the words 'are' or 'be' (as in this sentence). Take this example from a mobile communications firm:

> Representatives can be armed with the latest stock levels, delivery schedules and account details.
> Urgent orders can be entered directly on to the mainframe computer, ensuring immediate action.

You can rewrite this text to make it sound more immediate:

> Arm your representatives with the latest stock levels, delivery schedules and account details.
> Enter urgent orders directly on to the mainframe, ensuring immediate action.

If this sounds too bold or direct, you may want something more restrained or polite. Why not try:

> You can arm your representatives with the latest stock levels, delivery schedules and account details.
> You can enter urgent orders directly on to the mainframe, ensuring immediate action.

Sometimes people use the passive voice because they don't want to use the word 'you'. For some, the word is too friendly or insufficiently imposing. Remember that you are not trying to impress or intimidate the customer, merely to serve his needs.

You can't always avoid using passive verbs. Sometimes the sentence will look clumsier if you try to change it to an active sense.

BE SPECIFIC

Don't write generalities, especially in your introduction. Plunge straight into the facts. Take this first sentence in a newsletter:

> Pacesetting MPL Ltd transport initiatives have been the focus of government attention recently.

What does this mean? Several sentences later, we come to the real point: 'Government minister J. Smith has just toured our Whitehaven site to inspect revolutionary new road surfaces'.

WRITE PROPER SENTENCES

Here is a disjointed ad aimed at nursery shops:

> The new XYZ Child Seat.
> Your money-making multi-media superstar!
> A profit-making opportunity with XYZ's determined new initiative in developing the child safety seat market!
> Only 6 out of 10 children currently travel with suitable restraints!
> Only 1 out of 5 older children are secured with restraints!
> With its unique design features, XYZ's exciting new safety seat is a remarkable innovation.

This advertisement seems to have been made from slides left over from a sales conference. Its bullet points are cobbled together without any thought for the flow of ideas. Virtually every sentence ends with an exclamation mark, as if seeking to waken weary dealers from their slumber in the back row.

To make matters worse, those weary clichés, 'unique' and 'exciting', have been dragged into the text. There are also unnecessary abstract words such as 'initiative' and 'innovation'.

The text needs rearranging in a more logical fashion, and the reader needs help in moving through the text. The ad could have gone as follows:

> The new XYZ Child seat has many new design features. [List of features]. It's unlike anything else on the market, so you'll find it easier to sell.
> It's a big opportunity to make more profits. Here's how. [Proof.]

The market is still untapped: only six out of ten children travel with suitable restraints, and only one out of five older children is secured with restraints.

But we're helping to change that. Our extensive advertising campaign aims to develop people's awareness, and bring customers to your door and create sales.

WRITE THREE POINTS AT A TIME

As in the last sentence, copywriters often group their points in threes. Three-point sentences are neat, logical and easily understood. You can even spread the three points over three sentences:

> Over 60 per cent agreed that the new Volvo looked luxurious. Nearly 70 per cent thought it looked very relaxing and comfortable to drive. And almost as many described it as having a quality look.

For contrast, here is a meandering sentence that needs a three-point structure to make it comprehensible:

> As well as a big range of built-in features to cover everything for an organized life including: a diary that plans appointments as far ahead as the year 2050, an alarm so you don't miss important meetings, an address book with automatic search and tone dialler to dial telephone numbers for you, a calculator with power, root and factoral calculations, five memories, decimal point and format settings, all as standard.

Rephrased into three-point sentences, the text reads more clearly:

> The computer has a big range of built-in features to cover everything for an organized life. It has a diary that plans appointments as far ahead as the year 2050, an alarm so you don't miss important meetings, and an address book with automatic search and dialler. Also included is a scientific calculator with power, root and factoral calculations.

ADOPT A HOUSE STYLE

Consider issuing a style guide to staff about the use of

language. This would cover not only the use of the company name but commonly misspelled words and other points of uncertainty. For example, do your quotations specify all measurements in metric (with their imperial equivalent in brackets)?

TEN MISTAKES THAT REDUCE CLARITY
1 Don't write in capital letters
There is no need to write in capital letters. It is like shouting at the reader. Every capital letter is the same height, so readers find them more difficult to decipher. Here is an illegible trade ad delivered in capital letters:

BULK POT POURRI HAND BLENDED OF HIGH QUALITY. FRAGRANCES BLENDED FROM OUR FOUR SEASONS COLLECTION ARE:- SPRING DELIGHTS, SUMMER MEMORIES, AUTUMN SECRETS, WINTER BEAUTY. ALSO VICTORIANA ROSE, COTTAGE GARDEN, FIRE DANCE, WOODLAND SURPRISES, PEACH WHISPERS AND STRAWBERRY FIELDS.

Remember, just because the word is important to you is not enough to justify a capital letter.

Use capital letters sparingly and only for specific applications (not 'Get a free voucher when you spend £10 on baby clothes).

Use capitals for people's titles, but lower case if the title doesn't refer to anyone in particular.

2 Don't use foreign words
Include foreign words at your own risk. They will puzzle or humiliate your readers who don't understand their meaning.

3 Don't use quotations
Don't use quotations unless they are short and clear. Quotations from Shakespeare, Donne or (worse) Robbie Burns are meaningless to most people. It is tempting to use a quotation to add style to an upmarket brochure, but be warned: it can look superfluous and pretentious.

4 Don't put too much in one sentence
Some sentences contain too many ideas to be grasped at once. Here is a hotel advertisement:

> The Marlow House Hotel has consistently maintained a reputation for comfort, excellent food and service in the informal relaxing atmosphere of a spacious elegantly decorated country house.

This sentence contains six main ideas: (1) reputation, (2) comfort, (3) elegance, (4) service, (5) relaxing, and (6) food. The one sentence needs to be chopped into several. (Note, too, the number of abstract words that make the sentence feel spongy – there is no detail for the reader to grasp.)

Here is a factual sentence that got carried away in its excitement. Its thirty-nine words make it quite impenetrable.

> The 'Radblok' 40mm and 45mm thick '30' and 45mm and 54mm '60' doors are tested to BS476: Part 8:1972, are solid wood construction and the range embraces single and double door specifications with or without overpanels and viewing apertures.

5   Don't repeat yourself
Don't write about your 'comprehensive world-wide network'. If your network is world-wide, it is by definition comprehensive.

6   Don't overstate
Avoid superlatives and excessive claims. Words like 'very much easier' and 'much more simply' overstate your case and reduce your credibility.

7   Avoid trailing clauses
Every sentence needs to have a firm ending. Don't leave bits hanging off the end. The following example started as a three-point sentence, but somehow wasn't finished.

> The cassette and information pack gives details of this offer, explains how it will work for you, and tells you how you can try a course without risking a penny, with our fourteen-day money-back guarantee.

8   Don't state the obvious
Don't make statements of the obvious, and never prefix them with 'Obviously'. This implies that the point isn't worth

making – in which case you shouldn't have included it.

Never assume knowledge on the part of your readers. Any statement will be old news to 25 per cent of your readers, a useful reminder to 25 per cent, and totally new to the other half.

9   Don't write negatively

Don't say, 'You've probably never made real money'; say 'Here is your chance to make real money'. Don't say 'We haven't the widest range.' Say 'We have the right range for you.' Negative statements belittle and discourage the reader. Positive statements buoy him up, and make him favourably disposed towards you.

10   Avoid lists

No sentence should contain a list of more than four items. If you need to list more than four things, split them into separate sentences. Otherwise, the list will be too difficult to read.

The list can also be converted to bullet points, or put in a box on their own. Here, for example, is a recruitment ad with a lengthy list:

> The post will allow the holder to utilize their [*sic*] skills in design, in drawing up outline schemes and to fully document the tender and the inclusions and exclusions for presentation to the client and possibly producing working schemes in which the operatives will complete the installations.

(Note also how the writer cunningly decided to avoid using commas, in case this would aid comprehension.)

TEN WAYS TO IMPROVE CLARITY
1   Put important words at the end of the sentence

You can give important words greater emphasis by placing them at the end of each sentence, or before a punctuation mark. This writer knew what he was doing:

> Do your bit for Planet Earth. Ask your office supplier for Opti, the environment-friendly correction fluid. Non-

polluting Opti does not contain damaging chlorinated
hydrocarbons. The fluid dries on paper in seconds, and can be
used down to the last drop without thinners.

It looks simple. Yet in less sensitive hands the copy could
have been written with much weaker endings, missing the
most important points. Here is what it could have looked
like:

> The planet needs taking care of. So when you're at your office
> supplier next, Opti is the product to ask about. It is one of the
> most environmentally friendly correction fluids you can get.
> Opti is non-polluting because we don't use chlorinated
> hydrocarbons in the ingredients. On paper Opti quickly dries
> out, and it doesn't need thinners so every last drop can be
> used up.

2 Use headings
Avoid having acres of continuous text. Break up the text with
headings that tell the reader what is coming next. The
headings should list benefits in their order of importance.

3 Number your points
If the reader sees that there are ten points to absorb (as in this
section), rather than 3,000 words, he will absorb the
information more easily. This technique will also encourage
you to write more clearly, and force you to ask yourself,
'What points am I trying to communicate?'

4 Summarize your points
You can summarize the benefits in a coupon, in the PS at the
bottom of a letter, or on the back page of a brochure. Think
of the summary as saying to a friend at the end of a
discussion, 'The point I'm making is this … '.

5 Phrase it from the customer's point of view
Write everything from the customer's viewpoint. Ensure your
sentences focus on the customer's needs and interests. Don't
sell him your products – solve his problems instead. Use the
word 'you': it addresses the reader directly.

6 Don't start sentences with 'and'

Be cautious about starting a sentence with 'and'. Many older readers have prejudices about this, so while you can use it in brief advertising copy, it is best avoided elsewhere.

If one of your sentences starts with 'and', try joining it to the previous sentence with a semi-colon; and you'll find the effect is quite impressive.

Sentences that start with 'But' are slightly more acceptable, but you can usually join the two sentences (as here) without making the sentence too complex.

7 Be Bold

Don't be half-hearted. Don't say, 'We think you will enjoy this holiday'. Be confident about your products. Anything less will raise doubts in the minds of your readers.

8 Write Factually

One fact is worth a thousand generalizations. Take this fact: '72 per cent of all our reservations come from past clients or recommendations'. Wouldn't you book with that company?

9 Give your writing the overnight test

Leave your writing overnight. Look at it the following day, and you will see all sorts of errors. If you have time, leave the work for a few more days. In that time, your mind will unconsciously turn the subject over. When you come back to it, you will have a clearer idea of what you should be saying.

10 Let someone else see your draft

Show your writing to someone else. Find someone who doesn't mind hurting your feelings, someone whose opinion you respect. Ask him to comment on the words you have written, in terms of:

- How simple is it to read?
- How clearly are the points made?
- How interesting is it?

Listen to the comments with an open mind. If your reader finds the words are complicated, the chances are that other readers will feel the same way.

Don't ask someone to look at the writing if there isn't time to change the text. Don't ask for an honest opinion on a brochure that has already been printed.

CLARITY CHECK LIST

Is there a clear structure?
Have you used headlines and subheads?
Do sentences end with important words?
Have you got rid of abstract words?
Have you replaced long words with shorter ones?
Have you conveyed the sense using verbs rather than nouns?
Are sentences concise or rambling?
Are paragraphs short enough to encourage the reader?
Have you avoided passive verbs?
Are any words unnecessarily in capital letters?
Have you left any trailing clauses?
Have you included idioms?
Have you explained any abbreviations?
Are there any weasel words?
Are sentences linked?
Do any sentences lack main verbs?
Has jargon been excluded or explained?
Has the text been weakened by generalizations, statements of the obvious or slow-moving introductions?
Are all clichés banished?
Is the text general or specific, woolly or factual?
Are there any lists?
Is everything phrased from the customer's standpoint?

2 Create press releases that editors want

Costing just the price of a postage stamp, the press release is the cheapest form of promotion. By devoting time to it, you can save thousands of pounds from your advertising budget.

Editorial produces more enquiries than paid-for advertisements. That is because people read a publication for its news rather than the advertisements. And with newspapers and magazines spilling out millions of words each month, there is a lot of blank paper to fill. Many publications are chronically understaffed, and depend heavily on the press release for their news pages.

Press releases are easy to write: you only need simple statements. You don't need creative headlines or clever sentences, and you don't need artwork or colour printing. Quite the reverse: complicated releases obscure understanding and are less likely to be used.

The humble press release is a safe and useful way of communicating with the press:

- It allows you to decide which issue to promote, rather than having a journalist quiz you about other topics.
- It lets you select the right choice of words.
- It gives you a permanent record of what was said.

The editor benefits too. He gets clear information, and he doesn't have to worry about misquoting you.

But editors are busy people. A magazine editor receives thousands of press releases every month. The editor scans each release for just a second before making a decision. Most releases are consigned to the bin (editors have large bins). A minority goes into a tray for publication.

Successful releases have two merits. They are written in a journalistic format, and they are newsworthy. If you adopt this winning formula you will write releases faster and get more of them published.

USE A JOURNALISTIC FORMAT

Releases are written in a journalistic format for the editor's convenience. By following the rules, you put him in a better mood and make him react more positively to your story.

HOW TO LAY OUT A PRESS RELEASE

- Use simple words, short sentences and short paragraphs. If the editor can't understand what you are saying, he won't print the story.
- Avoid jargon. Don't assume that the editor and his readers will understand what the jargon means.
- Don't write more than three pages. If you must write more, add separate sheets as 'background notes'. Editors hate five-page releases about minor product updates. Check how many words you are likely to be given in your target publications. New products are rarely given more than 200 words.
- Write on only one side of the paper. This lets the editor see how the story flows, and allows him to cut up your paper.
- Use wide margins and double spacing. This leaves the editor room to write notes to the typesetter.
- Use a large typeface – not all editors have good eyesight.
- At the end of the release, put the word 'Ends'. This tells the editor you have at last finished. Then put a contact name and telephone number ('For more information, contact Jo Bradley on 071-500 0001). Many journalists work outside normal office hours. If they can't contact you in time to catch the deadline, they won't use the story.
- Put 'More follows' at the bottom of each sheet except the last. From page 2 onwards, put at the top right-hand corner of each sheet a short version of the headline plus its page number. For example, 'Smith appoints/2'.

An editor-approved layout will encourage the acceptance of your releases.

MAKE IT NEWSWORTHY

Every story has to contain news. Take a new laminating press. To you it may be a wonderful machine, but to the editor it is just another piece of machinery. If, however, you use it to make brain scanners, the editor is more likely to print the story.

Find an interesting angle, and you're guaranteed success. Here's a dull-sounding story: 'Company provides training for employees'. Change it to read:

Dawn Johnston wins top prize in new training scheme.

This has a better chance of being used – even though it's exactly the same story.

Every newsworthy story has three vital parts: the headline, the first sentence, and the subsequent paragraphs.

The headline should sum up the story in ten words or less. Don't make it clever or obscure. For an appointment story, 'Smith Ltd appoints new Managing Director' will do very nicely.

The first sentence should contain all the main points of the story. It should tell the reader *who* has done *what, where, why* and *when*. But don't let the sentence ramble on. It should be straight to the point, and it should not contain any non-essential information.

The first sentence of our appointment story might read:

Kevin Donovan has been appointed as Managing Director of Rochester-based Smiths Ltd, as from 1 January.

The subsequent paragraphs should add extra information in order of importance. Editors delete paragraphs from the end of the release, so don't leave vital news until the end. The appointment story could include:

- The man's previous experience and qualifications
- His age and marital status
- His home town and current home
- His hobbies and interests

You might also add a sentence about the company's products, and the new person's role in the company. But don't write a ten-page treatise for a story which will be condensed into two paragraphs.

DON'T ADD AN EMBARGO WITHOUT GOOD REASON

Old-style press release writers put an embargo at the top of their work in the form, 'Not for use before 7 p.m. 2 March'. This ensures that all publications get to print the story at the same time. It stops any publication from rushing into print before the actual event takes place.

The embargo is sometimes used to make an inadequate release look more important than it really is. This strategy rarely fools an editor and it could be counter-productive.

HINTS FOR GETTING ACCEPTANCE

Make it factual. Make your story specific by adding detail. A release about a new product should state what colours or sizes are available, and what the product is used for. If you are doubling the size of your factory, say how big the old factory was.

State the benefits: If the product is 20 per cent cheaper, or if it requires 50 per cent less servicing than similar machines, you should say so. Concentrate on the advantages to the customer – no one is interested in what advantages the product has for you.

Provide all necessary information: Ask yourself what a customer might want to know. What about after-sales service? What about spare parts? If you answer the questions in the release, it will save the editor ringing you or binning the release. Industrial companies often omit to add a price. You could give a minimum or maximum price, or quote the price for a typical configuration.

Avoid distractions: Don't mention irrelevant points:

A medical supplies company issued a press release about its new incontinence pads. The release started by introducing the products. Then it mentioned the company's new telesales operation. This was followed by news of a new sales office in Manchester. It then got side-tracked about the dignity of the elderly. By the end of the release, it was clear that the writer had forgotten the point of the release.

Add quotes. They allow you to make observations and add a human touch to the story. For example,

> 'Mary Benson has extensive knowledge of the hotel industry', said Jeff Greaves, the company's Chairman. 'This will help us to gain more business in that important market.'

Quotes allow you to give a point of view. They let you make a claim that can't be substantiated; they reflect the personality of the speaker, who need not be fully objective about his company's achievements. Quotes give you more freedom than ordinary editorial text, which must stand up to rigorous analysis. Here are some statements that could only be used as quotes:

- 'Together, our two companies are going to become market leaders,' say Mike and John.
- 'No one else can match our strength in tableware,' says the Sales Director.
- 'We have single-handedly pioneered the development of adhesives in the industry,' said Mr Ffoukes.

To summarize, if you want to make a contentious point, put it in quotes.

Always include a photo. Editors, particularly of trade journals, are often short of good photos to enliven their pages. They want lively, close-up photos, showing action. Instead they get boring photos showing line-ups of men in suits. They want crisp, sharp prints; instead they get fuzzy pictures taken by an amateur.

Write the release as it would appear in the magazine. Put yourself in the shoes of the editor. How would he write your story? He wouldn't be over-enthusiastic about the product. He would describe it in a factual way, summarizing its main benefits in a few lines. He would write it to the same length as other articles in his publication, and in a matching style.

DEVELOP AN AWARENESS OF GOOD STORIES
Every company has a number of potential stories, but they are rarely recognized because staff don't think like journalists. Aim to think in headlines. Every unusual order, every new recruit, every development in the company's history could be a good story.

Editors like articles with conflict or tension. That is why they don't print 'good news stories'. The media like 'Coals to Newcastle' stories (such as selling radios to Japan).

A company can often turn staff stories to its advantage. When staff raise money for charity, their company sounds philanthropic. It is worth telling the media about such activities.

PITFALLS TO AVOID
Here is one release that is destined for the bin.

> For over 100 years, the products of SMITHS LTD have been received with great sucess in the market, and its service has been continuously improved in an effort to ensure that their product range fully meets the requirements of the consumers. Following its remarkable adaptation to the consumer's requirement for modern styling, the company have decided to introduce a supplement to their already extensive range of attractive products; and as a result of an on-going programme of R&D, a unique range of stylish personal adornment accessories is being introduced by SMITHS LTD.

There are eleven major flaws in this release. See how many you can spot before reading any further.

1   It doesn't summarize the story in the first sentence. The release is announcing a new jewellery range, though you wouldn't know it.

2   Vague adjectives such as 'unique' and 'modern' add nothing. Most of them are meaningless puffs for the company. (One well-known company insists on putting the word 'exciting' in the first line of every press release, which may account for its lack of coverage).

3   Abstract words like 'adaptation' are difficult to understand. It is better to say 'the company has adapted'.

4   The release uses jargon. If you mean 'jewellery', don't say 'personal adornment accessories.'

5   The sentences are far too long. There are only two in the entire passage, where six would be better. The paragraph itself should be split in two.

6   Many of the verbs are passive ('is being introduced'). You can avoid this by turning the sentence around to read 'The company is introducing ... '

7   Plurals and singulars are mixed up ('The company have decided').

8   The company has put its name in capital letters. No publication ever puts the names of companies or their products in capital letters. Yet many companies persist in doing this. It is guaranteed to irritate the editor.

9   Words like 'requirement' and 'range' are repeated unnecessarily. A quick glance at a thesaurus would reveal several alternatives, which will prevent the text from sounding monotonous.

10   There are no details about price, size, colour or availability.

11   To add insult to injury, there is a spelling error. Did you spot it?

A better version of the same story might start:

Smiths Ltd has launched a new range of fashion jewellery in their fifty shops across the country. The colour coordinated jewellery comprises matching necklaces, rings, brooches and watches. Prices start at £5.99 for a brooch.
   The jewellery comes in five colours (pink, red, green, blue and yellow), and is made from translucent plastic. It is

designed for everyday wear, and is aimed at the 16 to 24 year age group.

'We've brought a bit of fun back into jewellery,' said Frank Manton, the company's Managing Director. 'And with such low prices, people can afford several different sets.'

TIPS FOR A BETTER RELEASE

Don't issue a no-news release: Some companies send out one press release a month, irrespective of whether anything has happened. The editor of one important trade publication bins all press releases from one firm, so tired is he of reading stories that start:

Price, quality and excellence – the hallmarks of ABC Ltd

When this firm runs out of puffery, it reviews existing ranges. A typical release is headed: 'Lintels to meet all purposes'. The practice should be avoided for 'news' releases. But it is acceptable if you send the story to a magazine that is reviewing lintels in a forthcoming issue. In such a case your release should be headed 'Lintel Review, 15 August'.

Don't add a date: Adding a date is unlikely to benefit you. Journalists like to know exactly when an event happened: they like to think that a launch happened this week. But by the time the release has been approved and appears in print, it is often weeks since the event happened. So it doesn't help to put:

A new range of videos was launched on 5 March.

It would be better to say:

ABC has just launched a new range of videos.

The only times to include a date are when:
1   You are inviting journalists to an event.
2   There is a major event a long way in the future.
3   There is a closing date for applications.

Don't say 'A company spokesman said'. In real life news, the journalist has forgotten to ask the name of the person he interviewed. If you want to add a quote, add the person's name. It makes the company sound more human.

Don't say 'The company claims'. In the real world, a newspaper adds the word 'claims' to cast some doubt on a statement. For example:

> The new drug will wipe out Aids within six months, claims the company.

Don't use negatives. They create a negative impression, and double negatives are even more confusing. Consider this example:

> The company will not ignore the needs of the market. It does not intend to miss being represented in Europe.

From reading this, many editors would think that the company will ignore the market and avoid Europe. It is always better to express action positively.

WRITING FEATURE ARTICLES

Longer length feature articles are more rewarding, because they let you discuss your subject in detail. You can offer to write a feature article by sending a letter to the publication, outlining the topics to be covered.

The publication may ring back to accept your offer. If so, they will set a deadline and a length (usually between 500 and 2,500 words). If you have a problem with the timing or length, tell the editor straightaway. When he first agrees to the idea he can accept a later date or a shorter article; but in four weeks time he will have a blank space awaiting your piece.

A feature article on your company will only be used if you are a market leader or an aggressive growth business. Smaller businesses have to work harder to get their name in print. Use your specialist knowledge to suggest a topic that will interest other readers. It should be a subject that hasn't been covered recently, and one that you are qualified to write about.

This isn't as difficult as it sounds. In your daily dealings with customers, you will pick up issues or concerns faster than the journalist marooned in his city centre tower block. Each industry has its own emerging problems. It may be prices, profitability, government involvement, unfair competition, Europe, safety or competing products.

> A car leasing company wrote an article warning fleet owners about the dangers of buying their cars by contract purchase.
>
> Though contract purchase gave fleet owners major savings, it was untested in law. If the Inland Revenue decided that contract purchase was unlawful, many companies would end up with a big tax bill.
>
> This article raised the company's profile and made it seem knowledgeable.

For local press the story must relate to the area, while a trade journal will require a technical slant:

> A software company told readers of a computer magazine about the use of software tools in the Harrier jump jet. Better software led to smaller hardware, and a precious saving in the weight of Britain's fighter aircraft.

Your article should help people or companies solve their problems. You may be able to offer advice or information. It might be on safety, training or financial planning. It might be on retail display, computerization or marketing.

HOW TO GET MENTIONED
Sometimes the article will be attributed to you. If this happens, you will need to write a 'Standfirst' to introduce the article. This is a short piece of text, usually one to two sentences long, which precedes the headline and summarizes the article. For example:

> As computing power grows, more and more bakers are linking their computers into a network. Mike Andrews of Catering Computers examines the options.

Many publications pretend they write all the articles. In such cases, you should ensure that the article contains enough references to your company, taking care not to overdo it. Add quotes from leading people in your company, and provide captioned photos that show your product.

HOW TO REVEAL THE BAD NEWS

There are times when you have to tell the press about bad news, such as redundancies or plant closures. If you don't issue the news, the media will soon find out and print an exaggerated version.

A 'bad news' press release should be designed to achieve minimum coverage, and be timed to miss the deadlines of the most important media. If the trade press has a Tuesday deadline, you can issue the story on Wednesday. Editors don't like printing week-old news, so your release will receive less prominence.

But in the bad news business there is a worse stage, known as 'Crisis PR'. This is when the media ring up saying they have heard that your chemicals have just wiped out Southern Europe.

It is tempting to avoid the press at times like this. But rather than saying 'no comment', it is nearly always better to give the press your side of the story.

The worst possible solution is to say, 'The matter is in the hands of our solicitors and I am unable to make any comment.' This merely confirms the company's guilt in the minds of the readers, and makes you sound distant and calculating.

In the interests of fairness, most publications will include your statement. Even if it comes in the final paragraph, that comment can be crucial in calming the situation. You can offer an explanation, an assurance that the matter is being investigated, or a promise that it will never happen again. These points will make the company seem less blameworthy.

Alternatively, you can go on the offensive. You can point out that 99 per cent of your production is fault free. Or you could dismiss the opposition as a minority or as people with a vested interest.

Timing is crucial. If a journalist rings up, find out when his deadline is. Don't make any comment over the telephone, especially if you haven't got the full details (or if you haven't a clue what he is talking about). Unless you are an accomplished politician, it is better to put your thoughts in writing, rather than spouting what first comes into your head. The difference will show in print. Tell the journalist that you will ring him back with a story, and set a time limit.

When you have ascertained the facts, fax your comments to the newspaper in time to meet the deadline. Write your comments in such a way that they can be quickly included in the story.

If you miss the deadline, you can write a 'letter to the Editor'. This should concentrate on the good news, rather than reminding readers what the problem was.

WRITING ABOUT THE ENVIRONMENT

Companies are now being questioned about the damage they might cause the environment, and any company can expect to be attacked by a pressure group. You should have your arguments ready and in a written form.

Explain all the points in your favour. Your products may be useful to society, and they might have provided innocent pleasure to thousands of people for two decades. There may be no viable alternatives, and you may be investigating other raw materials.

> The Peat Producers Association prepared a leaflet explaining the facts about peat-digging. It also sponsored academic research, arranged for an expert to tour local radio stations, and drew up a code of conduct.

THE 'QUESTION AND ANSWER' LEAFLET

If closing a loss-making plant, you might want to produce a 'question and answer' leaflet for the press. The leaflet should contain all the points that a journalist could ask.

Specimen question and answer briefing document
Q. Why is the plant being closed?
A. We are making losses from the products it produces. The total costs are £485,000 a year, while the sales are only £149,000 a year.

Q. Why is the plant making a loss?
A. The demand for such products is declining. At one time
    we sold a lot more. The product is a commodity, made
    by many other companies, and is sold at very low prices.

Q. Could the plant make other products?
A. No, the machinery is designed to make this one product.

Q. How many jobs will be lost?
A. The plant closure will mean a net loss of fifteen jobs. The
    plant employs twenty-five people, but we hope to
    relocate ten of them to jobs on other product lines.

Q. Are more redundancies to come?
A. No. There is a strong demand for our other products.

This briefing document can also be used for staff.

MAKING THE MOST OF THE NEWS
If your product is topical, you will find it easier to get
coverage:

> Following a spate of house fires which killed several children,
> a flame-retardant spray company gained valuable publicity. It
> told editors that the spray, when used on curtains and
> upholstery, gave people an extra thirty minutes of protection
> against fire. Several women's magazines mentioned the
> product, and the coverage brought the company extra work.

HOW TO GET STARTED
Start with a simple story, such as an appointment. Keep it
short, enclose a captioned photo, and send it to relevant
publications.

Don't underestimate how long it takes to get into
publications. A monthly magazine can take three months to
print your release, and allow four weeks for a weekly
newspaper. The editor of a monthly magazine is working on
issues as far ahead as six months, and he will have stopped
working on next month's issue several weeks ago.

Don't pin your hopes on getting a story into one particular feature. The publication may be inundated with material for it. Issue stories regularly, and you will have the pleasure of finding your stories in magazines when you least expect to see them.

Don't ring the publication to ask, 'Did you get my press release?' This is the one question that journalists hate. The answer will be: 'I get 100 releases a day. If it was usable, it's in a pile awaiting a future issue. If not, it's in the bin.'

GETTING BETTER RESULTS

There are many reasons why a story doesn't get used. A common explanation is that the publication received thirty appointment releases that month and had space for only twenty. Here are some ways that will help you get your stories printed.

Send out enough stories. The more you issue, the more will get printed. Business people are often too busy to write stories. They will frequently say, 'We aim to send out one release a month, but due to pressure of work, we haven't sent out any for the last four months'. Ensure that you issue at least one story a month. But don't send out a release for the sake of it.

Draw up a list of good stories. Target them at the press you want coverage in. Your local newspaper will want human interest stories about charity fund-raising and local drama, while consumer magazines will want to know about new products. Make sure everyone is involved in gathering stories. Make one person (the receptionist or the Marketing Manager's secretary) the central point for collecting stories.

Agree a time plan. Decide which stories are going to be released each month. Keep the lines of responsibility simple. Don't have committee meetings about press releases. Don't send the press release to several people for their opinions.

Don't assume you need Press Release paper. Companies often think that their story will look more impressive and confident on paper that says 'Press News from ABC Ltd'. While this is true to an extent, it can also look contrived. News is spontaneous, and formal press release paper never conveys that impression.

Releases often look better on an ordinary letterhead. It suggests immediacy and honesty. Journalists don't like using press releases. They see themselves as crusading sleuths, and rehashing a press release is hardly the stuff of investigative journalism.

Set up an efficient label system. Put the addresses of all the publications on to the word processor. Ensure they can be printed as labels at the touch of a button.

The labels don't have to include the Editor's name: you can simply address it to 'The Editor'.

Set up a production system. It takes a surprisingly long time to photocopy a batch of releases, staple and fold them, and insert them in envelopes. Make sure there is a production system.

Cast your net widely. Companies often send their releases to just three publications, those that they are familiar with. But if you seek out *Brad* or *Willings Press Guide* (found in most libraries), you will discover many magazines you have never heard of, all of which can bring useful sales leads.

THE BEST TOPICS FOR A PRESS RELEASE

Scan the press to see what company news is being reported. You will find it falls into distinct categories. The press uses certain types of news, and you should aim to supply it.

Most releases belong in one of the categories mentioned below. If you have a story that doesn't fit any category, it may not be newsworthy. Note, too, that many of the headings contain the word 'new' – a vital part of any release.

New product, new sales literature

Many companies launch new products without bothering to send a press release to their trade press.

Yet the trade press is likely to print the news of your new product, providing it sounds interesting. Failing to issue a press release is to do your product a disservice. If the editor decides not to print the story, you have only wasted the cost of a stamp.

The product doesn't necessarily have to be new. If you

have a little known product, you can write a press release about its virtues, and a trade publication may print the story. If the editor hasn't written about the product before, he may regard it as newsworthy.

You should always send the publication a sample of your product if it is inexpensive. If it is costly, invite journalists to phone you for a sample. They rarely abuse the offer. In nine times out of ten, a journalist who asks for a sample will write about the product.

When it comes to larger machines or a service business, you should offer journalists a demonstration or a visit to an installation. Some won't mention a product unless they have seen it in action.

Unusual product or company

The press likes to report on companies that have a fashionable product or an unusual niche in the market. It is also interested in a company with a long history, an unusual boss (especially a woman), or a company that is rapidly growing. So if your female-run snuff company suddenly finds its products back in fashion, you should be talking to the press.

New factory or investment

The opening of a new factory is in itself not very interesting (except to you and your employees). To get coverage, the factory may need to be expensive ('£3 million gobstopper factory opens'), or have a big output ('40 million gobstoppers a year from new factory'). Alternatively it could offer substantial employment ('50 new jobs to be created at gobstopper factory').

New division or restructuring

A restructuring is only likely to interest those people who are being restructured. However, you might use it to confirm the future of a plant ('New Runcorn fishfood division will spearhead company's growth').

The same applies to an acquisition, disposal or merger. It needs some facts to become a news item, and the scale of the story will determine whether a news editor uses it.

Record sales, exports, financial results
Public limited companies are obliged to report their annual figures, but there is no reason why smaller companies shouldn't use their annual sales as a way to get publicity (providing they are doing well).

You can summarize the year's highlights, mention the numbers of staff employed, and talk about your sales growth. You can mention new premises, new products or any other feature of the year. Use the opportunity to launch next year's plans as well.

New appointment, promotion
Since people are forever changing jobs, new appointment stories continually need to be written. To the outside world, the appointment story suggests that the company is successful, which is a good reason for writing the release.

Check the amount of space given to appointment stories. You will find that each person is given no more than four or five lines. You should write your press release to this length, though few companies succeed (try telling the new Finance Director he is worth only four lines).

Charity event, community activity, sponsorship or award
One distributor gained substantial press coverage by raising money for an incubator for a local hospital. Over the period of a year, the staff organized fun-runs, held sponsored parachute jumps, and collected money in the streets. For each event, the company issued a press release, which earned for the company a sheaf of press clippings.

Other companies sponsor industry awards. You can create 'Best Young Programmer', 'Hi-fi Sales Assistant of the Year', or the 'Northern Budgie Owner Awards'.

Promotional event
A firm of timber merchants celebrated the opening of a new branch in an unusual way. They invited a karate champion to officially open the premises by smashing down the front door rather than walking through it. The 'door' was a mocked-up frontage, but the event gained considerable publicity.

Competitions are another way to get into print. The secret is not to make them too difficult. Most people find competitions hard to answer, and have forgotten most of what they learned at school.

Case study or application story

If a well-known company uses your product to solve a problem, you should tell the press. The example below has an exotic location, a well-known end user and a dramatic application.

> A fume cupboard from ABC Ltd is helping the Hong Kong Police Department in its fight against crime. The unit is used for examining bloodstained clothing and other contaminated items from the scene of the crime.

The ideal case study shows readers how they can benefit by using the product or adapting it to their needs.

Celebrity visit

The popular press lives on a diet of celebrities, most of whom come from television or sport. So if you want press coverage for a shop opening, get a celebrity to perform the official ceremony.

The drawback is the expense, with few celebrities costing less than £750 for an appearance, and well-known personalities costing from £2,000. The simplest way to find a celebrity is in the *Yellow Pages* under 'Entertainment Agencies'.

Write to the media four weeks in advance, and remind them one week before the event. Tell the press *who* is coming, *what* he is famous for and what he will be doing, *where* it will take place, *why* it is happening, and *when*.

Don't rely on the press turning up. Your opening may coincide with the surprise arrival of Prince Charles in the area. Hire a professional photographer, and issue a press release after the event.

Use your imagination when it comes to celebrities. Father Christmas was appropriate for the December opening of a day nursery, and cost a lot less than a TV celebrity. The press release started:

> Father Christmas came early when he opened the new Toy Box day nursery at XYZ Ltd ...

On another occasion, William Wilberforce, the eighteenth-century slave trade opponent, opened a twentieth-century hairdressing salon in Hull (his native city), by being driven down the main street in a four-horse carriage. The celebrity was played by a member of the local drama society, and the carriage was hired from a wedding company. The story was on the front page of the local paper the following day.

Conference or seminar
A suspended ceiling contractor recently invited the Technical Director of a well-known manufacturer to give a talk on fire retardancy to a group of local architects and builders. His comments were reported in the trade press, and the contractor received free publicity.

If you want to get coverage, ask your speakers to talk on matters which are controversial or topical. Get a copy of the speech, and put it into a press release form:

> The trade is failing abysmally to counter competing materials, according to a leading industry spokesman. Speaking at a seminar held by the Bakelite Phone Company ...

Before going into print, remember that you can provoke hostility by attacking the industry. If you aren't ready to sustain an attack, avoid controversy.

Research survey
The press likes using research reports, because they provide factual new information. Many findings are based on dubious methods of collecting the information, but your data should be capable of standing up to scrutiny. You can stop one hundred people in the local shopping centre, or commission a professional research firm to carry out a survey.

Most large research companies also accept one-off questions on their 'omnibus' surveys.

For PR purposes, research should be designed to provide a headline. Your first sentence should carry a surprising fact, such as 'Eighty per cent of people don't mind paying more for green products.'

Be warned, however, that the national press may print the information without mentioning your company name.

You can also use research defensively, because market research answers always favour the questioner. Imagine your plastic bird bath company is under attack from conservationists who claim the bird baths threaten the environment by using non-renewable resources. You could ask two questions:

Question 1. Which of the following pose a serious threat to the environment?
——   Unleaded car exhaust fumes
——   Pumping raw sewage into the sea
——   Nuclear power
——   CFC aerosols
——   Plastic bird baths

Question 2. Should production of plastic bird baths continue in this town, assuming proper environmental safeguards?
——   Yes
——   No
——   Don't know

These questions are guaranteed to give you a headline that says 'Bird baths are "not a major issue", say Nuneaton people.' Or '95% think plastic bird baths should continue.'

Here are four other questions which will give a 95% 'yes' answer:

- Do you think birds enjoy splashing about in a bird bath?
- Would you like to attract more wild birds to your garden?
- Do water features add interest to a garden?
- Do we have a responsibility to help wildlife?

Reports

You don't need market research to write a report. Providing you have the information, you can write reports on issues that affect your customers.

- A firm of estate agents could use its seasonal sales pattern to comment on trends in housing.
- A trade association could write a report on the benefits of using its products.
- An insulation company could provide a report on the alternative ways of saving energy in the home.

Passing on this information will benefit readers, so it is likely to be reported favourably in the press.

PRESS PACKS

When booking a stand at an exhibition, you will be invited to supply press packs.

Before preparing your press pack, it is worth considering how it will be used. At the press office of any major exhibition, each journalist sees an expanse of press packs. He picks out the odd pack, leaving many untouched on the shelf. How do you get the journalist to select your pack?

The press are rarely impressed by luxury. Avoid a glossy corporate wallet. The best container is a transparent plastic folder which lets the journalist see the contents, and which excites his curiosity.

If the only words on a press pack are an embossed corporate statement, 'Market Leaders in Grommet Technology', the journalist is unlikely to believe that the pack contains anything newsworthy.

You could put the contents into a plain folder or A4 envelope, and add a sticky label on the front. The label should entice the journalist with newsworthy copy:

New biodegradable grommets launched by ABC Ltd
Stand J142

The first thing a journalist should see when he opens the press pack is a photo of something new. Behind the photo should be a press release about the new product.

Behind this you can add supplementary press releases about other, more minor launches. Don't include releases about existing products – journalists may think you are trying to hoodwink them into writing about old news.

A brochure, or a corporate profile on the company, is sometimes added. But avoid padding out the press pack with too much information. Two-inch tomes which look like a submission to a public enquiry give journalists a sinking feeling. An editor can tell just by weighing the pack that it probably contains little news.

WRITING PRESS INVITATIONS

Press invitations are best done as a letter with an attached reply form. The letter needs a simple, informative headline. This will ensure a busy editor grasps the purpose of the letter.

The letter should reveal some of the planned attractions without giving away the whole story. The reply form should make it easy for the journalist to respond. It shouldn't ask the journalist to add detailed or unnecessary information. Here is a simple invitation letter.

Dear Editor

Invitation to the press launch of a new range of toys

I am writing to invite you to a press launch for the new range of Toyland Toys. The event is taking place on 5 April 19XX at 11.00 a.m., at the New Theatre, Drury Lane, London.

At the launch we will be revealing Toyland's charming new Destructa Machines and Nuclea Armageddon Fighters. We will also be launching a secret new toy for the 4-8 age group. Lunch will be served after the presentation. I would be grateful if you could let me know whether you will be attending.

Yours sincerely

Andrew Henderson
Sales Director

Launch reply form

———   Yes, I will be able to attend the Toyland press launch.

———   I won't be able to attend the Toyland launch, but would like the information sent to me afterwards.

———   Sorry, I won't be able to attend the launch.

Name ————————————————————————

Publication ————————————————————

Please return this form to Toyland by:
- Fax (0749) 99001
- Letter to: Toyland Toys, Toyland House, London SW1
- Or telephone Jenny on (0749) 99002

3   How to write a compelling sales letter

Direct mail is fast. You can write a letter this morning, copy it at lunch-time, catch the post at 5 p.m., and get replies tomorrow morning.

It is also easy to evaluate – a letter either brings you orders or it doesn't. Once you know what percentage of recipients reply to your letter, you can keep sending it out until the response rate drops or you create a letter that gets a better response. (One office equipment company works its way through the *Yellow Pages*, from Abattoirs to Zoos.)

Unlike many other forms of promotion, direct mail is easily tested, and researchers have learnt what works. Now you can apply these lessons to your mailings to get better results.

MAKE USE OF YOUR LETTERHEAD

Don't use your ordinary notepaper for direct mail: adapt it to make a more effective piece of communication. The letterhead is the first thing people see when they open the envelope. They scan it for clues about the sender's identity and his reason for writing to them. Use the letterhead to start selling straightaway.

The most prominent words on the letterhead should be the company name and a selling benefit. Don't treat the letterhead like a tablet of stone – vary the message. If you want people to telephone, make the phone number visible. The address is less important: if you want people to reply by post, they will expect you to give them a reply paid envelope.

Fax and telephone numbers should be separated. Many letterheads give them equal prominence because the designer thinks it looks neater. But this practice serves to confuse the reader in his search for the right number.

The VAT number, registered office, and other useless legal information should be tucked away in small print at the bottom of the letter, or at the end of the final page. Some major companies even dispense with this information altogether.

Use the bottom of the letter, known as the letter foot, to sell. If there is printed information at the bottom of the letter, the eye will be drawn to it, particularly if it is in a different colour. So here is another place to conduct your selling. The letter foot is the ideal position to show membership of a trade association or a quality control mark such as BS 5750.

Don't use this letterhead for ordinary letterheads. It will be wearing for regular customers to receive such a forceful message every time they get a routine letter from you.

WRITE AT LENGTH

A three to four page letter often produces more sales than a one-pager. Yet most of us are embarrassed about writing long letters. We are taught to express ourselves succinctly, and at parties we know it's boring to talk about ourselves.

But although long letters look rambling, they serve a real purpose. The recipient needs a lot of information if he is to buy your product, or contribute to your cause. A short letter rarely gives him enough information to make him change his mind or alter his purchase behaviour.

This rule applies to most letters. Take the reminder from your local garage telling you that your car is due for a service. Rarely is the letter long enough. It needs to tell you:

- Why you should use this garage rather than any other
- How reliable and friendly the staff are
- How modern the equipment is
- The advantages of using a main dealer
- The risks of missing a service

A good rule in direct mail is: keep selling until you run out of sales points. By the end of the letter, the reader should know everything he needs to know about your product. Your letter should include all major benefits and cover every major objection you can think of.

But make the text relevant. There is no point in writing long letters just for the sake of it.

OFFER A FRIENDLY GREETING

The 'salutation' is the greeting at the start of the letter. The worst type of salutation is 'Dear Sir/Madam'. It tells the reader 'We don't know who you are, and we don't really care'.

Ideally you should address your letters to a named individual, and in many mailings this will increase your response rate. Some people must be addressed by name: the only way to reach every doctor in a surgery is to address each one personally.

But it can be costly and time-consuming, particularly if you are targeting companies where executives regularly change jobs. If you haven't got the individual's name, you will have to use a title. Business letters are often styled: 'Dear Production Director', 'Dear Computer User', or 'Dear Specifier'. This salutation tells the reader that the letter is relevant, and shows him you know about his interests.

Consumer mailings should not greet the reader as 'Dear Householder'. That doesn't distinguish him from any other householder. But 'Dear Parent', 'Dear Boat Enthusiast' or 'Dear Customer' tells the reader that the mailing is specially for him.

USE A STRONG HEADLINE

Put a headline at the top of the letter. Use the headline to communicate the main benefit. Make it easy for the reader: tell him why he needs to read your letter.

Keep the headline simple. The reader must be able to grasp it in one scan of the eye. Don't use too many words in the headline, like the publisher who wrote:

I WILL SHOW YOU HOW TO:
MAKE YOUR CUSTOMERS PAY UP PROMPTLY. SOLVE STAFF PROBLEMS. PUT-UP PRICES. WIN PROFITABLE BUSINESS. CUT BORROWINGS. REDUCE OVERHEADS. NEGOTIATE LONGER CREDIT.
AND ANSWER ALL YOUR FIRM'S LEGAL PROBLEMS. DAY OR NIGHT.

This 38-word headline dulls the mind with its endless list of benefits. The overpowering capital letters reduce comprehension still further.

Only the first word in each heading needs a capital letter.
All the other words should be in lower case unless grammar
demands otherwise. There is no need for this type of effect:

A Difficult Choice? There's No Choice If You Don't Subscribe
NOW.

Capital letters are the written equivalent of shouting at
your customer. It isn't nice and it doesn't work.

USE SUBHEADS TO SELL

Add subheads throughout the letter. These are smaller
headlines that tell the reader you are moving on to a new
point. Like every word in the letter, the subheads should sell
the product. Don't use dull words like: 'Styling' or
'Technology'. Try 'The luxury of Italian styling' or 'Wind
tunnel technology'.

Look through the headings in this book – they
communicate information or a benefit. Then compare them
with the headings in other information books. Dull headlines
often stem from laziness – the writer hasn't thought deeply
enough about his message.

MAKE THE OPENING POWERFUL

Give your letter a dramatic start. You have to gain the
reader's attention; he will have a lot of other things to do on
the morning your mailer arrives. Picture your letter being
opened as he hovers by the wastepaper bin. He scans the start
of your letter, his mind on something else. Your opening
must jump out at him and prevent the letter from being lost.

Like a good direct mail letter, each of the chapters in this
book opens in a dramatic way. Remember how, in the
bookshop, you flicked through this book, and read the first
words of a couple of chapters. Other books were competing
for your attention. So the openings had to work hard.

Find a glossy magazine, and look at how each article starts.
You'll find it begins with a challenging statement, an
interesting fact or a question – anything to get the reader's
attention.

OPENERS THAT SELL

Here are some themes for openings:

Challenge	(Do you know how many days your firm loses through sickness?)
Impressive fact	(We spend £64 million a year on bin liners ...)
Personal experience	(When recovering in hospital, I ...)
Knowledge of your interest	(As a keen gardener, you ...)
A story or case study	(When the Applejack Ice Cream company needed extra space ...)
A warning	(Your premises could be closed down tomorrow ...)
A special offer	(We'll give you a coffee machine free for sixty days ...)
A problem shared	(Does the rain come through your roof ...)
Trial	(Try this test. Dunk the attached card in your coffee ...)
Pose a question to which the answer is 'yes'	(Would you like to own a new BMW 5 series?)
Personal appeal	(You can lose ten pounds a week with our revolutionary new exercise plan.)
Dramatic statement	(This letter will save your life.)
Straight benefit	(A set of novelty teapots for just £14.95 each.)

Compare these openers with one from the market leader in personal organizers:

Dear Colleague

For every business, change and it's implications on efficiency represents a major challenge. Accessing key data, simplifying tasks and handling information; these are key areas where improved techniques can result in major benefits.

This opener manages to break most direct mail guidelines. It contains no benefits. It fails to grab the reader by his lapels. It

makes several statements of the obvious. It is full of dull
abstract words (like 'change', 'implications', and 'efficiency').
What's more, the salutation doesn't clearly define the reader's
occupation or interests, and the opening contains a
punctuation error – 'it's'.

ASK FOR WHAT YOU WANT

Many letters are slow in asking for the sale. If you want the
reader to buy your crockery, tell him so. If you want him to
take out a subscription, ask him to sign up. Don't leave it
until halfway down the page. By that time the reader will
have thrown away your letter.

Don't carefully prepare the ground by explaining about
your company's expertise and its tradition of quality. You
can't afford the wait. Plunge straight in with the benefit. Tell
your reader what you are offering him, and tell him why he
needs it.

SELL THE BENEFITS

Like every type of promotion, it's important to know what
exactly you are selling. More than just computer discs, lawn
mowers and insurance, you are selling reliability, a beautiful
lawn, and peace of mind.

Decide which is the most important benefit, and sell that
first. Then sell each of the subsidiary benefits in turn.

Phrase every point as a benefit, not a feature. Don't say:
'the computer runs at 12MhZ'; say 'The computer runs at a
very fast 12MhZ. That means you don't have to wait for
information to appear on the screen'.

WRITE FROM ME TO YOU

Direct mail is more personal than any other form of
promotional writing, which is one reason why it is so
successful. Take advantage of this intimacy by having one
customer in mind when you write.

Address the reader as if you were sitting beside them, in
their home or office. Use the word 'you' frequently, and if
you want to be really personal, you can talk about 'me' as
well. Most organizations feel more comfortable using 'we',

and the word 'I' is often reserved for a letter from a famous personality, perhaps on behalf of a charity.

Check your letter for sentences that use 'we', and see if you can convert them to 'you'. This will emphasize the benefits to the user. Instead of saying, 'Our shirts are smart', say 'You'll look smart in one of our shirts'. Change 'Our duvets are warm and comfortable' to: 'You'll feel warm and comfortable in one of our duvets.'

WIN THE READER'S AGREEMENT

It is important to get the reader nodding as early as possible. Find some common ground – it will set the tone for the rest of the letter. Try ideas like, 'Exporting to America has damaged even the largest companies', or 'Reliable cleaners are hard to find'. But don't write statements of the obvious (see the personal organizer example above).

UNDERLINE IMPORTANT WORDS

Use underlining to identify the most important words. This helps the reader who scans your letter, seeking the main points. Use underlines sparingly, and only underline relevant words or clauses.

INDENT TO EMPHASIZE

Another way to focus the reader's attention is by indenting a paragraph.

> An indented paragraph stands out from all the normal paragraphs and attracts the eye. You can use it to emphasize special information, to add an example, or to include a benefit which doesn't relate to the rest of the text.

By breaking up the text you make it easier for the eye to fix on the detail, and the letter looks easier to read. But keep indentations for special thoughts. If you use an indent for a minor point, the reader will feel cheated and he will lose confidence in you.

Each page can take two indented paragraphs. Any more than this, and the letter will look like a jumble of words, especially if it is decked out with underlinings, subheads and all the other trappings of direct response.

USE A LEGIBLE FORMAT

On A4 paper, your text should be 150mm wide, with a 30mm margin on either side. Common sense will tell you that a letter whose text spreads to the edge of the paper will looked cramped and difficult to read. A letter with abnormally wide margins will look equally odd.

A four-page letter is better printed on a sheet of A3 paper and then folded to A4. This makes the letter simpler to produce, and it is easier for the reader to hold.

Use 10 point text. A smaller type-face will reduce the legibility of your letter. Many readers have imperfect eyesight.

LET THE STORY UNFOLD

The letter must flow properly. Guide the reader gently from one point after another, and he won't realize you are detaining him longer than he intended. A logical flow retains more readers for longer.

To flow properly the letter should obey two rules. Firstly, the sentences should be linked; and secondly, the ideas should develop in a logical order.

To link sentences and paragraphs, you should use joining or contrasting words, or words which encourage the reader to travel deeper into the sentence (see chapter 1).

As for the logical sequence of ideas, you can't simply put your thoughts on paper and then send out the letter. Sales points have to be carefully structured. Start with a strong opening, followed by a series of connected major benefits. Follow this by minor benefits, interspersed with case studies.

Your letter can move from simple ideas to complex ones. Or it can move from benefits that affect everyone to those that affect fewer people.

Try setting down your letter in bullet-point form. This makes it easy to check whether the points follow a logical order, and whether every point is included.

DON'T OVER-PROMISE

Don't make claims that won't be believed. It is a mistake to use a case study that achieved a 500 per cent increase in sales if the reader is unlikely to believe you. It is better to quote a more modest figure.

Nor should you make promises you can't keep. Many letters end by saying:

> I will ring you next week to see if you would like to try one of our new golf trolleys.

This makes depressing reading for the 98 per cent of readers who don't want a golf trolley. Here, says the reader, is another rep I'll have to fight off.

Worst of all, this promise (or threat) is rarely carried out. In few cases does the writer actually telephone. So the reader views the last sentence with scepticism.

Look at the facts. You can send out 1,000 letters a week, but you can't ring the same 1,000 people the following week unless you use a telephone marketing agency. In that case, your letter should say, 'One of my staff will ring you'. Either way, don't say you'll phone people until you have worked out how you will achieve it.

GET THE READER TO ACT

By the end of the letter, the reader has read all the benefits, and become progressively more interested in your product. Now he says 'What do I do next?' You must tell him clearly what to do.

Every letter needs a paragraph which prompts the reader to act. The paragraph should stand on its own and be clearly marked. Don't complicate the issue by providing a lot of alternatives. Tell the reader to:

- Ring me now for a demonstration
- Fill in the reply paid card
- Attach your business card to the coupon
- Scratch the card to see if you have won
- Send £15.95 to the address below
- Ask for a technical representative to call

ADD AN INCENTIVE

Try giving an incentive. This will improve the offer, and overcome the reader's in-built inertia. Here are a few examples.

- Reply by 15 September, and we'll give you a free pocket calculator
- If you order volumes 1-4, we'll give you volume 5 free!
- Buy during the promotional period, and get 15 per cent off.
- This 10 per cent discount is only available to club members. So join now.
- There's a free menu planner with every order.

REASSURE THE READER

Give the reader the confidence to pick up his pen. Show him he can't lose. Tell him that if the product doesn't work he can have a replacement or a refund. Tell him you won't cash his cheque until the goods are despatched. Or tell him you won't bill him for ninety days.

Make the guarantee big and bold, and print it in a different colour. Put the guarantee in a 'bank note' frame to make it look like a legal document.

MAKE IT SIMPLE TO ORDER

Make the ordering process as simple as possible. Consumers rarely have notepaper, envelopes or stamps handy, and business people don't like to have their purchase routines altered. So if you can provide a reply paid card, a telephone ordering service, or a 'Bill me in thirty days', you will boost the response rate.

SIGN OFF IN A FRIENDLY WAY

Direct mail letters usually end 'Yours sincerely'. The strict rules of grammar say that non-personalized letters should end 'Yours faithfully', but this has an old fashioned ring to it. (If you are selling traditional crafts, 'Yours faithfully' might be appropriate.)

Some companies insist on adding the words 'On behalf of

ABC Ltd' above the writer's name. This sounds formal, even threatening. It is not recommended.

To make the letter sound friendly, you should include your Christian name rather than your initial. And it is worth including a friendly title. Sign yourself 'Sales Manager – Northern Region', and you will remind the reader that you are trying to flog saucepans. But 'Customer Liaison and Service Manager', conveys a benefit – your company clearly cares for its customers to employ someone with a title like that.

USE A PS

As the reader picks up a letter, his eye skips all over the page, looking for sections that are easy to read. The PS stands out. Separated from the main text and placed below the sender's name, it is easy to spot.

The PS seems to say, 'Oh, I nearly forgot. There's something I should add before I run to the post office'. The PS demands to be read, and research shows it is a powerful place to put an important point.

Sadly, the PS is often abused. The writer finishes his letter and thinks, 'I need a PS, because all direct mail letters are supposed to have one'. He can't think of anything to say, so he summarizes a sales point he has already made:

PS   Remember, this directory is the most comprehensive that
      money can buy.

The word 'Remember' is a give-away. It shows the PS contains nothing new. There are times when it is worth repeating a key benefit, but the PS deserves something better. The PS should be reserved for a 'just remembered' benefit, a sales benefit kept until last:

PS   The directory has a special new section on wholesalers. It
      lists all the products they stock, and it'll save you lots of
      time.

MAKE IT A PACKAGE

You can mail people more than just letters. The more creative the package, the higher the response rate is likely to be. Starting with simple ideas, you can include a brochure or leaflet that lets you convey the benefits of your product in glossy colour.

You can send a sample of your product. Or you can include promotional items which will last longer than the letter – wallcharts or coffee mats, for example.

Some companies include gimmicks for extra impact, such as pop-up origami. Others include a scaled-down product, or a dramatic enclosure (a key, an apple or half a £5 note).

But however sophisticated the package is, it will need a reply device – normally a reply paid card – to make it easy for the reader to respond. And this is what we turn to next.

A REPLY DEVICE BOOSTS RESPONSE

Reply paid cards save the reader time and effort, and tick boxes simplify his decision-making. If you can print the reader's name and address on the reply card, you'll make it even easier for him to reply. In fact, the best reply card doesn't require the reader to do anything other than push the card through a letter-box.

Having got your reader to the point of replying, there is a moment of hesitation when he stops reading your letter and picks up the card. The flow is broken, and he is confronted with a different piece of writing. At this point he has to commit himself, and he hesitates.

This is a dangerous moment, so you need to reinforce all those positive feelings by restating the benefits on the reply card. Many consumer cards start with a religious affirmation from the reader:

> Yes! I want my name to be entered in the free raffle. Please send me my free catalogue.

Business people are less likely to be anxious about signing a post card. But they *will* worry about unwanted visits from reps, and they won't want their name added to yet another direct mail list. You can allay their fears on the card, by saying:

> No salesman will call, and completing this card puts you under no obligation to buy.

For business-to-business reply cards, the tick boxes could include:

—— Please send me more information
—— Please send me a sample pack
—— Please ask a representative to call

You may also want to collect some useful sales and marketing information, such as:

Current computer system ....
Type of boat owned ....

The reader is doing you a favour by filling out your form. So don't ask for information he may not want to give at this stage (such as his telephone number or the size of his sales force).

If you want people to place an order, you will need an order form or a coupon, plus a reply paid envelope. Keep the order form as simple as possible, and lay it out clearly. To reduce indecision, you should limit the reader's choice of colour or size.

The reader may not be in a position to buy yet. Perhaps his stationery supplier is letting him down, but he isn't sure whether a new supplier would be any better. He doesn't want you to pester him with phone calls. But he *is* interested in knowing a little more and being kept up to date.

So your coupon may need to distinguish between enquirers with immediate needs and those who might become customers some time in the future. Your coupon might read:

—— My need is urgent. Please phone me.
—— Please put me on your mailing list, but don't contact me yet.

Some types of sales are more contentious than others. A managing director might not want his employees to see a coupon that says:

> Yes! I want to know more about relocating my company to the Highlands of Scotland.

If you are selling sensitive products or services, provide a reply paid envelope or a card that can be sealed in half.

TRY A LETTER WITHIN THE LETTER

Some consumer mailings include a smaller second letter. This is often inside an envelope carrying the words, 'Open this envelope if you decide not to buy the encyclopaedia'. The second letter usually contains an extra set of benefits, or an endorsement from the Managing Director or a celebrity. The second letter will add to the cost of your mailing; a test will show whether it is cost-effective.

WHAT SORT OF ENVELOPE?

Direct mail agencies like putting promotional copy on the envelope. They say it encourages the recipient to open the letter. The truth is, they can't bear to see all that unused white space.

Putting advertising copy on the envelope has one disadvantage. It warns people that the envelope contains direct mail. Only direct mail people send envelopes saying 'You could have just won £1 million'.

So if you want to put a message on the envelope, it should be credible and sincere, rather than bland and breezy. The message should not tell the whole story: it should aim to stimulate people's curiosity. But there is always an exception to every rule: one catalogue company puts its best offers on the envelope. Why waste the white space?

The envelope must reflect the quality of your product. If you want to position your company as serious or reliable, you might be better off investing in better quality envelopes with a discreet logo, rather than shouting on the envelope: 'Win two new cars!'

SPECIFIC TYPES OF LETTER

The most disappointing letters are the ones sent to people who have responded to an advertisement. These letters are often typeset, giving them an impersonal look that real letters never have. The text is short and uninspiring. Here is what you can expect to receive.

Dear Sir/Madam

Thank you for your recent enquiry about our services. I now have pleasure in enclosing a selection of brochures.
    We hope to have the pleasure of remaining

Yours faithfully
FOR AND ON BEHALF OF
INTRANSIGENT HOLIDAYS LTD

Marsha Hughes
p.p. A.G. Morris
Managing Director

This letter isn't really trying. The writer isn't interested in his customers and he has an old-fashioned style. From the text of the letter, you can't even tell what product he is selling.

The letter has been printed with the Managing Director's name and title, but it has been signed by Marsha, who does all the real work. The p.p. suggests that the Managing Director likes seeing his own name but can't be bothered to sign his letters. If Marsha signs the letters, why not let her do so in her own right? Why not give her a special title for sending the letters? How about Customer Response Co-ordinator?

The text of the letter could have been much more gripping:

Dear Holidaymaker

Superb holidays – for less than you'd pay elsewhere

This is where your holiday begins. Just weeks from now, one of our Boeing 737s could be whisking you away to a *sunny shore* of your dreams.

We have hand-picked holidays in the best places. Many of them you *won't find in any other holiday brochure*. Why? Because we take more care in selecting our holidays. Our senior staff have *personally visited* every single hotel and beach. And if they wouldn't stay there, it doesn't go into our brochure.

We also offer a no-quibble *money-back guarantee*. If your

holiday doesn't come up to your expectations, we'll refund the full amount.

So where will you go this year? Take a look at the new Poros holiday on page 17. Your hotel has saunas and a gym, and the vast sandy beach is rarely busy.

Look at the *special interest holidays* we've lined up on page 24. As well as getting a tan, you could learn to scuba dive or go pony trekking.

To book your holiday, ring our Holiday Line on 071-110 0001, or send off the booking form.

Yours sincerely

Nick Quibble
Holiday Planner

PS   Book within 7 days of receiving this letter, and you'll receive a free 112-page guide to your chosen destination.

This letter starts selling as soon as it is let out of the envelope. It tells the reader what makes the company different from other holiday firms. It tells the reader what is new this year. It sells the dream of a perfect holiday. It builds confidence and reassurance. And it has hardly started.

The letter could get one of last year's holidaymakers to talk about the wonderful time she had. It could get a hotel manager to say what a discerning company Intransigent Holidays is. Or it could include other benefits – perhaps a child-minding service, free coach trips or free throw-away camera.

Letters should always sound friendly and charming. Too many are curt, not because the writer is intentionally rude, but because the letter is brief. If your letter is short, it will sound brusque even if you think you are sounding efficient. Writing flowing relaxed letters comes naturally to a few people, but most of us have to make a conscious effort.

THE PRICE INCREASE LETTER
Here is a standard price increase letter:

Dear Customer

This is to notify you that as from 1 October the prices of all our products will be increased by 8 per cent. We are sorry to make this increase, which is forced on us by rising raw materials and wage costs.
Yours faithfully

A. Blenkinsop
Finance Director

This letter misses an opportunity. It fails to tell the customer that the products are still value for money; and it fails to remind him of several sales points. Here is a better version, in which we get the bad news out of the way as soon as possible.

Dear Mr Paulson

A price increase – but still great value for money
I'm sorry to tell you that as from 1 October the prices of all our products will be increased by 8 per cent. This increase has been forced upon us by rising raw material and wage costs.

But our products are still excellent value. We have held our prices for over a year now, and with inflation running at more than 9 per cent, this price increase means we are actually *cutting our prices* in real terms.

What's more, if you order during the next month, your goods will be despatched at the old price – making a worthwhile saving.

Have you seen our new nursing home products?
We've also launched some great new products recently. Our new *high chair* now comes in three new colours, and at £155 it's great value for money. And have you seen our new high-tech *incontinence pads*? They're extremely comfortable, and they're available in five different styles.

Please ring our sales desk on 071-008 1010 if you would like to place an order, or find out more about our nursing home range.
Yours sincerely

Andrew Blenkinsop
Finance Director

The letter could go on to tell the reader about the wide range of quality products and the reliable 48-hour delivery. It could invite the reader to ask for a catalogue or request a salesman's visit. It could also tell him that the Financial Director is available for complaints or comments at all times.

This letter gives more than just information:

- It presents a specific image of the company.
- It proves the sender is sufficiently interested in the customer to communicate with him in detail.
- It shows the sender cares about offering a good deal.
- It reveals that the sender is a friendly sort of person.

If everything else was equal, the customer will buy from the writer of the second letter rather than the first. In other words, the second letter has added sales value.

SEVEN WAYS OF IMPROVING RESPONSE
1 Include an endorsement
Endorsements are powerful persuaders. They are 'unsolicited testimonials' – approving comments by impartial observers.

An endorsement can be provided by:
- A customer (preferably named)
- An academic
- An opinion former (such as a leading politician, lawyer or doctor)
- Market research ('90 per cent of our customers have used us for more than five years', or 'More companies use our system than any other')

2 Put it another way
There may be other ways you can express the benefits of your product. You can tell the reader what he will miss if he *doesn't* buy your product ('Without this Controller, you'll face increased electricity bills and less control over your energy use').

You can also compare it with other products which may be less sophisticated, more complicated, less attractive, bulkier, or more difficult to install.

3   Involve the reader

It is vital to keep your reader involved all through the letter. You must stop him from throwing away your half-read letter. You can do this in a number of ways. Ask him rhetorical questions ('What would you do if you lost your job?'). Put questions that he himself might ask ('So how much does it cost?'). Or give a vivid example:

> When Bleak Brothers bought our system, they halved their accounting costs overnight.

Talk about his industry ('If your shoe repair equipment has to be replaced too often, you'll become less competitive ... ').

Share your hopes with him. Confide in him. By the end of the letter, you and he should be friends. You might imagine that this approach isn't appropriate for (say) a high street bank. But why not? Here is part of a letter from a bank manager asking for your company account:

> Like you, I'm running a business. I've managed the Altrincham branch for three years, so I know something of the problems that local businesses face.
>   Like you, I have staff to manage; and so I share your concerns. Take the monthly payroll – a big headache for most companies. Did you know that we offer a staff payroll service?

You can also involve your reader by shocking him or by being blunt. For example;:

> Your pension is vital for a satisfying retirement. If you don't agree, stop reading now.

4   Justify the deal

If you're making a bargain offer, explain why you're doing so. Readers are inclined to fear the worst. A money-off deal implies shoddy merchandise, while a free trial implies that the reader will be stuck with the product.

So be open with your reader. Tell her that by selling more

you can reduce the price. For a free trial offer, tell her: 'Only by trying the product can you see how well it works'.

For an introductory offer, tell her the truth: 'We want you to get used to our product in the hope that you'll carry on buying it'.

5 Overcome objections

Write down all the things that could worry the customer about your product – all the things that could stop her buying it. Then decide how you would overcome each of these objections. For example:

Objection	Response
Can't afford it now	Easy payment plan
Need to compare it with others	Provide a comparison chart
Don't want to pay this month	Pay nothing for thirty days/until September
Not sure whether the colour will match my furnishings	Try it in your own home for a week
It looks complicated	Customer helpline
It may break down	Nationwide chain of service agents
I don't know anything about your company	Celebrity endorsement

6 Add pictures

Your letter isn't restricted to words. You can include pictures:

- A photo of the sender, captioned 'Mike Thompson, Managing Director'.
- A drawing of the problem the reader encounters – or its solution. Again, this needs a caption to make the drawing plain.
- A blank 'notebook' for the reader to write down his requirements.
- A cheque showing how much the reader could earn.
- A lifestyle illustration showing what the reader can aspire to.

- A box telling the reader about the company's size and location.
- A 'before and after' illustration.
- A photo of a satisfied customer, next to his testimonial.

The drawback of such devices is that they make the communication look less like a 'real' letter. Every market is different, so there are no hard and fast rules. Test a letter with an illustration against a text-only letter. See which works best.

7 Test your letter

Direct mail professionals never stop testing. That is because direct mail is such a precise skill. Each different letter produces a different response rate. And the higher the response, the more money you make.

The secret is to change only one thing at a time. Change more than one thing in a mailing, and you don't know which of them caused the difference in response rate.

Start by changing the headline. Mail half your sample the original headline, and send the other half the same letter with your new headline. Check if the response varies.

Quite small changes have an effect on the response. You can add underlinings, delete paragraphs, or alter the order in which the benefits appear.

If you continue to test, each succeeding letter should produce a higher response. In practice this doesn't always happen because products change, letters wear out, and competitor activity affects the market.

Changes to test in direct mail
Speed (slow down the text, or speed it up)
Length of letter
Use of adjectives
Underlining
Frequency of using 'you', and 'we'
Personalize (writing to a named individual, as opposed to a title)
Headline
Subheadings

Length of paragraphs
An emotional appeal compared with a practical appeal
Different incentives
Different response devices (or even the absence of a response device)
Additions to the mailer (a leaflet, or a supplementary envelope for those who are hesitant)
Type of paper, size of paper

MISTAKES TO AVOID IN DIRECT MAIL
Each of these mistakes is taken from actual sales letters. None are invented.

Don't write on both sides of the paper when using staples. It is difficult to read the back of stapled sheets, and the print on the reverse side is visible through all but the heaviest paper.

It is however, all right to use both sides of the paper when you are printing a four-sided letter on to a single sheet of paper.

Don't use typeset print. It makes the letter look less spontaneous. Use only a typewriter face. Letters are supposed to be newsy and instant, and typesetting destroys that illusion.

Don't use justified type, the sort that has smooth right-hand margins. In a letter it makes the text more difficult to read, and it loses the homespun look that makes letters so powerful.

Don't use italics except for occasional emphasis. Because they lean to one side, italics make the print swim before the reader's eyes.

Don't write 'Date as postmark'. It adds nothing to the letter. It merely tells the reader that he is dealing with an old-fashioned and bureaucratic company that can't be bothered to write a personal letter. Many direct mail organizations' letters leave out the date altogether because it gives them more flexibility. If the letter is undated, it doesn't matter if the mailing is delayed for a few days.

Don't waste subheads. Use them to sell benefits. A heading such as 'Lindar Associates' is quite meaningless.

Don't delay in making the offer. Here is a letter that never gets around to saying what it wants you to buy:

Dear Business Colleague

As someone who relies on the telephone and needs to ensure that all phone messages reach you quickly and accurately, you've probably already considered the advantages of installing an answering machine, but until now there hasn't been a suitable system.
They have either been too expensive, too complicated to use or not practical enough to suit your needs precisely. That's why we at British Telecom used our unique understanding of your needs to design the Robin.

Note also the 40-word sentence which takes up the whole of the first paragraph.

Don't assume your reader knows you. One recent letter said 'As you are probably aware, we already offer a vast range of services to you the manufacturer'. The reader had never heard of the firm, so it was a rather presumptuous statement.

Don't use unnecessary words. Don't say 'the building and specification market' if you mean 'building'.

Don't over-claim. Don't invite readers to see you' at your 'Head Office', if only one office is shown on your notepaper.

Don't let spelling errors slip through. After the letter has been through the spellchecker, get a human being to read it. That will prevent such errors as 'We offers top quality merchandise'. A major tourist attraction wrote:

Indeed it way Henry VIII who spent lavishly to transform the castle form a fortress into a luxurious Royal Palace.

Don't put your company's name in block capitals whenever it is mentioned. Capital letters are the literary equivalent of thumping the table – it doesn't create the right impression. Here is a letter that puts the product in capital letters:

Dear

In response to your enquiry I have pleasure in enclosing further information on our range of **WALL BEDS** and Complimentary Cabinets.

Our **WALL BEDS** are designed in two heights and twenty-three finishes. It is not possible to supply a price list but if you would care to telephone us, we would be pleased to discuss your individual requirements and give you some indication of cost and delivery.

Don't simply type 'Dear', and follow it with a handwritten 'Mrs Wright' (see the wall bed example above). This tells your reader she has received a standard letter to which her name has been added. If you want to prepare a stack of pre-printed letters, you have two choices. You can leave the salutation line blank and write the whole greeting by hand ('Dear Mrs Wright'). Alternatively, use a standard salutation such as: 'Dear Architect'.

Don't use jargon. What, for example, is a 'seek and find service' referred to by a French property expert?

Don't make statements of the obvious. Don't tell people things they already know.

Don't be half-hearted. No reader will be impressed if you say, 'Our mailer will be supplied on request'. But you will set hearts racing if you say:

Just phone for our informative brochure. It's free, and it's packed with vital information about Australia.

Don't write long sentences. Here is a 39-word sentence from a company that is, unbelievably, selling Model Letters:

> To help you ensure that every letter you or your colleagues write is well-phrased, well-presented and above all gets results, there is now a source of hundreds of tried and tested model letters you can draw on.

Don't overuse direct mail devices. If your letter is choked with indentations, underlines and bold words, nothing will stand out. By emphasizing everything, you emphasize nothing.

4 *Dynamic sales literature*

Leaflets and brochures must be designed from the reader's point of view. That means they must have a logical structure. The information must unfold in the right order. Start by analysing what the reader needs to know. You can do this by assessing the order in which the reader's questions will flow. For a holiday brochure, the reader might put the following questions:

Question	Brochure section
1 Which country shall I visit this year?	Introduction – Spain, France and Greece
2 What part of the country shall I go to?	Introduction to Normandy
3 At what hotel do I want to stay?	Selection of hotels
4 What amenities or attractions are there?	List of amenities
5 What will it cost?	Price/date box
6 What dates are available?	Price/date box
7 How do I get there?	Information about flights
8 What assurances do I get in case anything goes wrong?	Guarantees
9 How do I book?	Booking form

The same process applies for a business-to-business brochure. What questions will the buyer want answered, and in what order? For a lift manufacturer the sections might go as follows:

Question	Brochure section
1 What sort of company is it? What does it stand for?	Corporate statement about safety and reliability in lift manufacture
2 How big should the lift be?	Our range of lifts – one for every need
3 How will it fit?	Our design skills – we can fit lifts anywhere
4 What space is needed?	Technical drawing, showing space required
5 How will it be maintained?	Service: engineers, call-out, guarantee
6 Can I have an estimate?	Address, telephone number, contact name

This system ensures that all readers will pick up the most important points about the product. Put the simplest information first to encourage more people to read the brochure.

Don't get carried away by your own enthusiasm, especially when it comes to technical features. The customer may be more interested in dramatic photos rather than the details of how the product works.

WHAT FORMAT BROCHURE DO YOU NEED?
The standard leaflet is A4 size, which is convenient for filing. Fold A4 in half and you get A5, which is ideal for smaller consumer brochures. Use two concertina folds on a sheet of A4 and you get a leaflet that works well for small hotels, financial services, direct mail, and in-store leaflets. Bear in mind, however, that an unusual size or shape will help your brochure stand out.

NUMBER OF PAGES
Having decided the format of the brochure, the main points to be included and the types of photos, you should have a clearer idea how many pages will be needed. Try doing a rough layout, using the size of paper you think is most suitable for your brochure. Some points will need just a

sentence, while others may take a whole page. Remember to allow room for photographs or illustrations.

Single sheet leaflet: A single-page leaflet gets straight to work. On the front is usually a photograph of the product. The copy is restricted to a headline and perhaps a strap line or slogan. On the reverse is technical information, plus the company's name and address.

Some companies try to make the leaflet work harder, by including text on the front of the leaflet as well as the back. This looks cramped, and cheapens the effect.

Four-sided leaflet: A four-sided leaflet looks a little more generous, and allows you to convey more information. Its front page normally has just a headline, photo and logo, leaving the inside spread for text. The back page can be left blank or used for technical information.

Stapled brochure: These brochures provide 8, 12 or 16 pages, or any other multiple of 4. If you have a range of products, or if your product is complex, you will need the extra room that a stapled brochure provides. (Printers called a stapled brochure 'stitched'.)

Folder: Use a folder if you have several leaflets, each on a different topic. Folders are ideal when you regularly supply quotations, or when you need to include technical drawings or data sheets. You can use a folder when the information is likely to change or expand. Use it also when different customers don't need all your leaflets.

When new products come along they may be added to the folder. And when old ones are deleted, the leaflet may be discarded without wasting all the literature.

DESIGNERS' DISEASE, AND HOW TO SPOT IT
Designers' disease is rampant in brochures and leaflets. Check for these symptoms:
- The text is printed over a logo or a faint photographic image, which makes it difficult to read.
- The text is laid out in solid rectangular blocks.

- The printing is typeset in 'artistic' but illegible typefaces (often a curving script).
- The text is right-justified – it has a smooth right-hand margin which looks nice but reduces legibility.
- Colour washes are draped across the text, so that the background changes colour at a different part of each line.
- The text is printed in lilac ink on yellow paper, making it impossible to read.
- The headlines are printed without capital letters.
- The headlines have extra space between each letter, making it impossible to read without moving your lips.

The cause of designers' disease is simple: many designers design for other designers, rather than for the client.

No one ever reads leaflets which suffer from designers' disease. The reader sets them aside to be read at some future date, which never comes along. Providing you don't mind this, you can enjoy the prestige that such literature conveys.

If, however, you want customers to read your information, and if you think the words are important, you should be on your guard against this problem.

Some designers deride conventional design. But you should remember that design, like the text, should be so transparent as to be invisible. Nothing should come between your customer and his understanding of your products.

THE FRONT COVER

There are two options for the front cover. It should either contain a benefit, or it should be thought-provoking. Both options encourage the reader to pick up the brochure and open it.

Many companies use the front cover of their brochure to list the products they make. This is particularly true for multi-product companies.

Here is the front cover of a leaflet that is offering to insure your car phone. On the front cover are the words:

TRIPLE OPTION
INSURANCE SCHEME
Loss and Damage
*
Extended Warranty
*
Combined Cover
*
Arranged by Marigold Insurance

This is a typical failure of imagination. The company couches its service in technical jargon. There are no benefits. And the statements don't identify the real nature of the sale, which is two-fold:

1   We'll replace your carphone if it is stolen.
2   We'll mend your carphone if it stops working after the 12-month warranty expires.

Hidden in the small print are some important benefits. The insurance company will:
● Replace your carphone straightaway
● Agree the replacement over the phone
● Take care of all the administration
● Arrange to have the work done at your local garage
● Help you stay in touch with your office and your customers by getting you back in communication quickly

So what should the leaflet say? We want the motorist to pick up the leaflet and read it. So we concentrate on the single most important point – in this case, the possibility of theft. The second benefit (repair when out of warranty) can be mentioned inside the leaflet.
The cover should have an illustration of the problem: a car with a broken window. The headline should say:

CARPHONE THEFT IS RISING
If your carphone is stolen, we'll fit a replacement within 24 hours

This leaflet will sell probably four times as many insurance policies – not because it is clever, but because it understands the reader's needs, and because it communicates the benefits more effectively.

CONTENTS PAGE

A list of contents is useful in brochures of eight pages or more. Make the table bold and separate it from the rest of the text.

Don't cram too much into the contents. List only the most important points. It isn't necessary to list everything that appears on each page.

Use the contents page to sell the brochure. Don't use boring words like 'Introduction' or 'Model 961'. Pick out the most important sales point from your introduction, and use that as the heading.

Try using different colours for each section, or use cut-out tabs. Both these points will encourage people to open the brochure.

Points to be included in a brochure
- Product features and benefits
- Styling, sizes, variants and colours
- Case studies, application stories
- Applications
- Accessories
- Care, cleaning
- Safety
- Guarantees
- After sales and service
- Corporate information
- Location

Other items are usually provided in a separate brochure:

- Technical information, specification
- Operating or installation instructions
- Price list, conditions of sale
- Stockist list
- List of clients

Not every brochure will use all these points. Use this check list to ensure that nothing important is left out.

You may need more than one brochure. Some companies separate their glossy sales leaflets from their simpler assembly instructions. Other firms keep technical literature separate.

DESCRIBING THE PRODUCT

List all the features and benefits of your product. Include every reason why the reader should buy your product.

When drawing up the list of features, add the words 'which means that ... ' after each point. Then complete the sentence. For example, 'The crisps are made from an original recipe, which means that ... they taste better, and contain no artificial additives' (You don't need to add the words 'which means that' on every occasion. They are simply a means of identifying benefits.)

Here are the features and benefits for a speed-boat engine.

Feature (facts about the product)	Benefit (which means that ...)
3 litre, 220 hp engine	Fast
Weighs 450kg	Good power-to-weight ratio gives extra power
Diesel engine	Fewer moving parts, engine low maintenance, more mpg, cheap fuel
Indirect ignition	No fumes, low noise
Two drives	Suits big and small boats
Easily accessible engine	Servicing is simple
Glow plug preheat	Trouble free starting
Computer designed	Vibration free, smooth ride

Remember that the purchaser is not always the user. So there may be more than one benefit for every feature. Take this child car seat brochure:

These different positions will make the journey more comfortable for your child and consequently more restful for you.

In describing the product, you don't have to use plain statements. A company that makes thorn-proof clothing might want to describe a shepherd in torrential rain on a lakeland fell – snug in his raincoat.

SIZES, VARIATIONS, COLOURS
Summarize all the possible variants, in a table if necessary. State what each is suitable for, and suggest ways in which the product can be matched or co-ordinated.

SATISFIED CUSTOMERS
Provide a case history, application story, or an 'unsolicited statement'. It shows how other people have successfully used the product.

CORPORATE INFORMATION
You may want to tell readers about the quality of your management and your company philosophy.

LOCATION
Your company's location can be used as a selling tool, by showing how close it is to motorways, airports or London.

If you export, to what countries of the world do your products go to? This will earn you respect.

TECHNICAL PERFORMANCE
The technical details are usually placed toward the end of the leaflet. For clarity and neatness, they are often presented as a table. They could include strength, fire resistance, safety, acoustics, and durability. Add guarantees, appropriate standards, and quality control marks. If you offer technical advice, here is the place to mention it.

COMPANY HISTORY
Customers will be less interested in the history of the company than you are. So don't include a history unless there is a good reason for doing so.

Histories should start with the most recent events, and work backwards in time. The exception is the date of founding, which may be mentioned first.

The history should sell the company – its success, its heritage, and its influence on the industry. The text should bring out the sales points rather than serving as a record.

THE CALL TO ACTION

Your leaflet must tell the reader what to do when he reaches the end of the leaflet. Provide an application form or a reply paid card.

AVAILABILITY

Where can readers find the product? This requires a list of stockists or branch depots.

CLIENT LIST

For a service company whose clients are likely to change, the client list is often printed as a separate sheet and inserted loosely into the brochure. It is often printed in one colour, so that it can be cheaply updated.

OPERATING OR ASSEMBLY INSTRUCTIONS

Assembly or installation instructions must be easy to understand, and should be accompanied by clear illustrations.

Instructions often miss out important stages, or condense the instructions too heavily. If in doubt, ask someone unconnected with your industry or family to assemble your product, and see how they do.

PRICE LIST AND ORDER FORM

The price list is usually a loose-leaf insert because it needs regular updating. The order form should have a serrated edge if it forms part of the brochure. This will encourage people to tear it out.

The price list and order form should be as simple as possible. Avoid any complicated tables or unnecessary questions.

A leading car ferry company asks customers to calculate the length of their vehicle in metres ('including roof top luggage'). Few drivers will have a tape measure handy, or will know where to find the information in their instruction manual.

Add the date of issue or period of validity, and if you are running a promotional offer, include a date on which the promotion ends. Add any information about ordering such as:

- Packaging charges
- Delivery charges
- Insurance costs
- Delivery time
- Quantity discounts
- Telephone 'hotline'

Also include on the order form your company's name, logo, address, telephone and fax number. Repeat this information on the back cover.

CONDITIONS OF SALE

Avoid a lengthy 'conditions of sale'. These are put together by solicitors rather than marketing people, and are very unfriendly. Imagine walking into a shop and deciding to buy a carpet. Instead of being delighted at winning a sale, the salesman launches into a ten minute disclaimer, absolving the shop from any responsibility whatsoever.

The law will probably take precedence over your conditions of sale. And if the product doesn't work, you will have to replace it or return your customer's money.

Try to reduce the length of the 'conditions of sale' – and try to simplify the jargon. Set your solicitor a target: 50 per cent of the existing length.

DEALER BOX

The dealer box is the blank rectangle at the bottom of the back page in which the dealer can add his rubber stamp. This personalizes the leaflet to the dealer and allows direct-sell firms to reward organizations who instigated the deal (credit card companies use this device).

TECHNICAL LITERATURE

Technical leaflets needn't be boring. The engineers, architects, and programmers to whom you are selling are also human beings who read popular newspapers. A technical brochure is also a statement about your company style and values. So if you have to invest a little more money on good photography, nicely designed layouts, better quality paper and well thought-out copy, it will be money well spent.

Technical literature is a vital marketing tool in industries where the product has to perform properly (aerospace, for example), or where back-up service is important. Technical literature reassures the specifier. For him it is the proof that the product works, and that it is suitable for his needs.

The content of technical literature is often similar to sales literature (a description of the product and its uses, and so on) though it is usually given more precise, formal headings. Technical literature is more restricted in content and format. But it still allows you creativity.

Be cautious about using advertising copy in technical literature. It is acceptable when it refers to a specific benefit (such as heat resistance or ease of use). But avoid vague claims. Many specifiers are irritated when advertising and technical copy are mixed together.

Unfamiliar terms should be listed in a glossary, or explained the first time they are used.

Ensure that your technical literature has a 25mm filing margin so that no information is lost if the leaflet is punched for filing in a ring binder. Pre-punched leaflets help the buyer.

Illustrations should be clear and simple, and diagrams or dimensioned drawings aid comprehension. Add graphs and tables, giving each a clear caption. Include an index at the back if the brochure is more than thirty-two pages.

If you put information on the spine, make sure that it reads from left to right when the brochure is lying face up. This will ensure that the title is the right way up when the brochure is on a shelf.

Topics for a technical brochure

Description – what the product is, and what it does

Range list/product selector – shows all the possible sizes and shapes

Samples and colours

Design data

Performance – strength, fire, acoustics and durability. Includes appropriate standards and test certificates

Applications – explains under what conditions different products may be used

Specification – helps the buyer to state accurately what he needs

Sitework instructions – a guide to installation

Operation and maintenance – instructions for use. Repair and servicing

Prices and conditions of sale – availability, packaging, ordering and delivery

List of suppliers

Technical services – planning services or advice on product use

References – examples of the product in use

FILING MARKS

Add a filing mark if this is standard industry practice. Apart from being useful to the filing clerk, they make the brochure look more professional. Their absence suggests that the company doesn't really understand its market.

Quality marks are also vitally important selling tools – they reassure clients about your company's skill and reliability. They are evidence that the products or services are of the highest standard.

If your company has BS 5750 and a similar quality mark, show the logo because it will be instantly recognizable to the customer. Show too any trade associations you belong to.

HOW TO WRITE ABOUT SERVICES

The services offered by hairdressers or skip-hire firms are difficult to quantify. So they need to talk about other benefits, including speed of delivery, reliability, excellence of service, quality of staff, problem-solving approach, versatility, customer orientation, breadth of experience, and contacts.

Endorsements are ideal for service companies, because they substantiate the brochure's claims.

Invisible benefits
Academic reports written
Ancillary services
Awards
Caring
Company ethos or corporate culture
Creative
Customer hotline
Dedication
Dynamic
Efficient back-up services (receptionists, secretaries)
Guarantees
Hard-working
Honest
Innovative
Insurance
Integrity
Long-established
Mould-breaking
Papers delivered at conferences
People oriented
Previous successes
Proposals and reports – quality
Reliable
Research quality, number of patents
Royal warrant
Staff quality, numbers or qualifications
Structured to align with customer's organization
Support services efficiency
Sympathy with customer's problems or needs
Understanding of customer's market
Well-known customers

SIXTEEN WAYS TO MAKE YOUR BROCHURE MORE INTERESTING

1 Decide what you are selling

Before you rush to describe the products, pause for a moment. Analyse what your customers are buying. Parents aren't just buying a toy, they're buying entertainment, ten minutes' peace, education, playground status or part of a collection.

Homemakers aren't buying a sofa. They're buying comfort, luxury, or a place to relax after the children have gone to bed. They may be buying a spare bed, or a co-ordinated furnishing scheme.

2 Add an incentive to turn the page

Add a flash on the front cover. Tell the reader that there is something to interest him inside the brochure. It could be 'Special Offer – See Inside', or 'New designs'.

3 Include a letter

Print a letter on the inside front cover. People find letters irresistible because they are a friendly form of communication.

The letter needs to carry your letterhead, have a proper salutation ('Dear Cat Lover'), and needs to be signed by a named individual.

The letter can direct attention to a new product, it can pledge good service, or it can invite the reader to telephone in the event of a complaint.

4 Make it useful

Put helpful information in your brochure. Provide metric to imperial comparisons, a summary of fire regulations, or hints on colour schemes. They will encourage your reader to keep the brochure, and refer to it more often.

5 Add an interview with the boss

An interview with the boss can be used to emphasize the company's quality, service, innovation, environmental awareness or growth. The boss can speak with a directness and eloquence that is denied a copywriter.

Agree in advance how much room the interview will take. Allow no more than one page. Make sure the interview is stringently edited, to prevent it from taking over the brochure.

6 Alter the shape
Don't feel constrained to use A4-size paper except for technical literature. Even technical brochures can use odd-sized paper, providing you are willing to accept a few complaints.

Try tall, extra slim leaflets. Try leaflets that fit a personal organizer. Try leaflets that are cut in the shape of a circle. Remember that odd shapes will affect your layout and increase your costs.

7 Get stuck in fast
Not everyone wants to be educated. Not everyone wants to know the manufacturing details of your product. So don't waste time telling them about things that don't convey a benefit. Take the start of a leaflet for a hay fever remedy:

> Hay fever is an allergic reaction which occurs in people who are particularly sensitive to pollen or spores released into the air by trees, grasses or moulds. Pollens released in spring are usually from trees, whilst in the summer, flower, grass or weed pollens are released. In the autumn the symptoms are usually caused by pollen from autumn flowering plants and the spores of some fungi.

This feels like a dry lecture on natural history. Sixty-six words into the leaflet and the reader is saying, 'Yes, well that's all very fine, but what are you going to do about my hay fever?'

The leaflet needs to get closer to the reader, starting with:

> If your eyes are itchy, your nose is running and you can't stop sneezing, you've probably got hay fever.
> Over 6 million people suffer from hay fever every year, making it impossible for them to lead a normal life.
> But now there's a new remedy …

All the information about spores and moulds can be put in a separate panel titled 'What is hay fever?'. That is where people with the time or interest can learn more about their condition.

8   Use headings to clarify
Headings help the reader through the brochure. Use them to separate the main points. The headline should offer a benefit, not a product feature.

Brochures don't need an introductory headline. The text can stand on its own, inviting the reader to get straight into the brochure. In less successful brochures the first headline is often a clumsy 'Introduction' or 'About ABC Ltd'.

9   Add atmosphere
Don't be aloof from your reader – let him share your feelings. Brochures can be dramatic. A gas-fire brochure should talk about rainswept winter evenings. A leaflet about a chauffeur hire service should silently whisk the reader through crowded London streets.

10   Make photos work
Clarify your text with photos or illustrations. Use each photo to illustrate a point. Aim for close-up photos, photos which demonstrate the product, or photos taken of the product in action.

Then explain the point in a caption beneath it. Photos in brochures affected by designers' disease always lack captions. Treat the photo as a sales aid, and remember that the reader will look at the photo first. Take advantage of his receptiveness.

11   Add graphs or charts
Graphs illustrate trends much more clearly than figures alone. Use a graph if you want to show that your heaters put out even heat during the day, or that your unit trust has consistently outperformed the rest of the stock exchange. But remember to explain what the graph means, and label each line clearly. Don't make the graph too complicated, and don't show too many lines.

12   Talk about your reader's needs

Start by talking about your reader, not yourself. Here are the first words in a brochure from a design consultancy:

> Communication is a complex process. We were formed in 1969 to help our clients deal with that process by providing a complete design, writing and production service ... The last 20 years have brought us work from over 300 companies, many from the construction world, others from a broader spectrum of industries ... combining to give us a powerful pedigree in a variety of disciplines ...

This is the bar-room bore in print. The company is more interested in telling you about itself, rather than telling you how it can solve your problems.

13   Give directions

Every brochure must be organized to help the reader. People like to flip through the pages, so they need guidance. Provide clear signposts throughout the brochure. It may be obvious to you that page 4 is about accessories, but does the reader realize that?

Each page should have a major heading. It helps the reader find the pages he wants to read.

14   Include questions and answers

Pose typical questions a reader might ask, and then answer them. Every new customer has uncertainties. What happens if the product doesn't work? Who can I return it to? What if I can't understand one of the knobs? Your questions show you are aware of the customer's concerns, and they make you seem a friendlier organization.

15   Make a special offer

Give your reader a free attachment, a discount for ordering from the leaflet, or a trial sample offer. This may be your only opportunity to sell your product to the reader for a long time, so make the best use of it.

16   Show the factory

If you show the factory in your brochure, use it to sell the product. Don't mention the factory just because it cost a fortune to build. Ask yourself which aspect of your factory would most interest your customers. Imagine that you are taking a customer on a tour of your factory. What would you show them?

A wide-angle view might show the scale of your works. You would say, 'This two-acre factory can produce up to eight million containers a year.' The customer will say to himself, 'This is a large and impressive company. They will be able to meet my needs.'

Show him your R&D department, where staff are measuring recently made products with advanced equipment. You will say, 'Our products are made to close tolerances', and your customer will think: 'They manufacture to high standards.'

You introduce your customer to Fred, who has worked for the company for twenty-five years. You say: 'Fred is a real craftsman; he enjoys his work. He cares about the products he makes.' The customer will say, 'Their quality must be good'.

SPECIAL TYPES OF LEAFLET

Next we look at literature which needs special consideration – range leaflets, sales promotion leaflets, case studies, and stuffers.

Range leaflets

A range leaflet contains a large quantity of products, such as books or small parts, with a short description of each. Some range leaflets become off-putting because of the quantity of detail.

You can break the text into numerous small sections to give the eye an easy entry into the copy. Try emphasizing points of interest. Pick out new products with the word 'New' and add extra text about it. Or put new products in a separate box.

Draw the reader's attention to others by adding a flash saying 'Bestseller' or '100,000 sold'.

Add a special feature article. This could be written by an expert in the field. For example, a leaflet on car maintenance books could have an article on cost savings through DIY car care, and be introduced by a well-known racing driver.

Sales promotion leaflets

Sales promotion leaflets are designed to get extra short-term sales or added trial, by giving the customer a special offer. The offer might be 20 per cent extra product, a competition, money off, free credit or a free gift. With this type of leaflet, you need to emphasize the benefits of the free gift or the prize.

Competitions need to be simpler than many business people imagine. Most people have limited knowledge outside the needs of their own life. So make it easy. The more people who read your leaflet and enter the competition, the more chances you have of selling your product.

Consider carefully before using tie-breakers. The traditional question goes: 'Say in an amusing or original way why every household should have a ... '. This will stump the average person whom you want to enter. It will, however, attract professional competition entrants, whose smarmy alliteration rolls off the tongue faster than any professional copywriter.

Tie-breakers are designed to avoid the threat of legal action from running an illegal lottery. But every week local newspapers run competitions where prizes are awarded by being first out of the bag.

If you want the reader to send away for something, add a coupon. It is easier for the reader to respond, and ensures that he provides all the information you need (size and colour, for example). Try to keep the coupon simple.

Get rid of boxes saying 'For office use only', unless they are absolutely essential. Make it clear which parts of the coupon must be completed by the reader. Shade them a different colour, and put crosses where you need a signature. But don't ask for a signature unless you need one for a bank.

Sales promotion leaflets also need a last date of entry. This is to stop entries coming in for years afterwards. Add 'offer available while stocks last'. This avoids an open-ended commitment to free products.

Financial reports

Financial information is obligatory in the Annual Report and Accounts. But few customers see this document, and a balance sheet is meaningless to most laymen. So more companies are now producing information for employees.

If you can demonstrate regular sales growth each year, the data can be presented as a bar chart. However, once you start issuing the figures, you are bound to keep producing them. In so doing you create a hostage to fortune. If your next year's figures are slightly down, you create uncertainty where none existed before.

You may also want to show important ratios, such as return on assets, or return on turnover. If presented as a bar chart with five years back data, your company's direction is clearly visible.

You may also include interesting articles about certain aspects of your activities.

Environmental issues

People are keen to know about a company's stance on green issues. So if you can boast any progress in this area you should capitalize on it. 'Greenness' can take many forms. It could relate to your policy on company cars, your attempt to reduce energy use, your donations to environmental organizations, or the creation of environmentally sound products. These items will add life and colour to your literature.

Social reports

Some major companies now give information about social indicators as well as the traditionally reported and legally required financial information. Your literature partly exists to convince employees, investors and your community that you are an attractive and socially desirable firm.

Most of this information can be presented as a bar chart, showing the last five or ten years data if you possess it. If you haven't, now is the time to start.

Information for a social report

- How many people work for you? How has this changed over the last five years, and why?
- What proportion of employees are women at each main level in the company (production, clerical, professional and managerial?) If the percentages decline in direct proportion to job status, your company will not be alone.
- How many UK suppliers do you support, and what is the value of your purchases from them? This is particularly relevant if your parent company is foreign.
- What percentage of the 'value added' goes to employees, shareholders, government tax, and re-investment in the business? This is a useful chart because it will probably show that most of the money goes to employees (contrary to popular belief).
- How much money does your company donate in sponsorship (to the community, the arts, sport, and political donations)? If the figures don't look very positive, now is your chance to change your policy.
- How much is the company spending on training? How many people are being trained, and in what way?
- What is the length of your employees' service? This information can be broken by percentage into bands from 'less than five years' to 'over fifteen years service'. These figures are only relevant if your employees tend to be long serving.
- What do your employees earn? If you pay well, or if many of your staff are highly qualified people doing skilled work, you can show the percentage of employees by salary band.
- What age are your employees? This information is only relevant if you want to prove that you hire lots of young people, or if your employees are smoothly graduated in age. This information would be presented in age bands.
- What jobs do your employees do? If you want to boast how many of your people are oriented to sales or R&D, then show the figures.

A social report tells the world that the company is striving to be a good employer.

Case studies

Case studies are useful because they tell a story. This makes them more readable than ordinary advertising leaflets.

You have to explain the solution (at least in outline) within the first few sentences. Otherwise the reader will read through the text, asking himself 'Why am I reading this? What is the point they are trying to make?'

Structure of a case study leaflet

- The problem and its solution.
- Background to the situation, location.
- The benefits that the solution provided.
- Quotes by the client.
- The specific products or services used.
- Other aspects of the job: time taken, contractors used. This can be used to mention benefits such as speed of work.
- Other services or products provided by the company.
- The company's name, address and telephone number.

How to lay out a case study

The best case studies name the client company. This gives added realism and drama – it becomes a real-life story. You can strengthen it still further by identifying a key person in the client's company (its Managing Director, Finance Director or Transport Manager).

Case studies work even better when they use quotes from the client. This shows that the client is willing to say favourable things about your company.

It is often best to write a statement that fits the sense, and then give it to the client, saying: 'We were looking for words like this.' It will save your customer time and effort. It will also prevent him from anxiously trying to write witty sparkling words – the sort that would win him a toaster in a local newspaper competition.

Stuffers

Stuffers are the small leaflets that are either pushed through letter-boxes, stuffed into mail order parcels or inserted into magazines. They are normally small in size – often DL (A 4 folded twice) or A5 (A4 folded once).

They must be cheap enough to issue in large quantities, but of sufficiently high quality to enhance the product. There is no point in producing a leaflet that makes people think your products are shoddy.

The cover must encourage the recipient to open the leaflet. It needs a dramatic message or photo. Inside, the text should convey the benefits, whether it be cleaner carpets, more attractive clothes, or draught-free windows. It must have a bold layout and an easily understood message. The back cover must tell the reader what to do next, and there should be a tear-off reply paid card.

The recipient may regard the stuffer as an irritant – it makes her hall floor look untidy, and it unexpectedly falls out of glossy magazines. So it has to work hard to attract the recipient's attention.

MISTAKES TO AVOID

1 Don't write too much

In today's television age, people are less used to reading. Many people are too busy to concentrate on one brochure for long. Garage mechanics won't wade through pages of text. Nor will housewives at a supermarket, nor a director on his way to a meeting. So keep it brief, and use lots of pictures. Some people, such as architects or designers, are very visual. They respond to pictures rather than words.

There are exceptions, however. Where people are deeply involved with your product, they will be keen to read every word.

2 Don't overlook customers' worries

Ask yourself whether you have answered your customers questions? A widely distributed double-glazing leaflet fails to talk about installation. Who will install the windows? Will the fitters be careful? Do they have any qualifications? What happens if a draught develops some time after the job is completed?

3 Avoid repetition

Here are some words from a brochure advertising a personal organizer: 'a unique, totally relevant management information ... versatile, totally integrated system ... infinitely adaptable ... portable, practical and infinitely flexible'.

This company has a penchant for stringing adjectives together. It doesn't work in a brochure. The reader tires of seeing the same words thrown up.

4 Don't use jargon

Don't assume that the reader has a detailed technical knowledge. Spell out all abbreviations the first time you use them. Don't use jargon (within the same trade, people have different words for the same item). Explain all technical points. If your machine has a 12 per cent dwell angle, what is its role?

Try this sentence: 'Our forward looking personnel practices help validate our key company belief in RESPECT FOR THE INDIVIDUAL.'

This probably means, 'We respect the individual, and our personnel policies prove it.'

4 Don't write long sentences

Here's a regional electricity company that got carried away. The sentence has thirty-nine words, including six main verbs and four 'that's'. It should be chopped into two.

> We're so sure that you'll find that this is the best way to pay that we have agreed that your bank can give you an immediate refund if an error has been made in the debiting to your account.

5 Don't reduce legibility

Don't use white text on a black background. Although it looks impressive, it is difficult to read. Keep to conventions unless you have a good reason for breaking them. Start sentences with capital letters (if that sounds obvious, many brochure headlines start with lower case letters).

Justified text (which has an even right-hand margin) is often difficult to read. So are italics.

6 Don't oversell

Don't start each paragraph with your company name. The repetitive appearance of your company name looks like overselling. In particular, avoid mentioning your company name in the first three words of the text. Nor should you put the name of your product in capital letters.

7 Don't include dates

Your brochure will be expensive to produce, and it needs to last. So don't use any dates in the brochure. Once the date has passed, the brochure looks out of date. Examples of dates are:

- 'See us on stand 101 at the H&V Show, NEC 15-16 July 1992.' This should only be put on short-term promotional material.
- 'A joint venture laboratory is due to be completed in late 1992.' Simply cut out the date: 'A joint venture laboratory is due to be completed.'
- 'The project was completed in December 1990, three months ahead of schedule.' Again, cut out the date: 'The project was completed three months ahead of schedule.'

A photograph that shows vehicle registration plates will date the brochure. It will also convey the wrong impression if the photo is supposed to demonstrate how modern your fleet is. Take the photographs in such a way that the number plates cannot be seen.

The exception is the sales promotion leaflet, where you must add the final date for entries.

8 Don't write half-sentences

A half-sentence lacks a main verb. Here is one about a new bank account:

> With instant access to our friendly Banking Representatives and financial specialists 24 hours a day, 365 days a year.

The sentence is part of some greater whole. But this is of no benefit to readers whose eyes skip around the brochure. They won't want to refer to the previous paragraph to find out the first half of the sentence.

5   Newsletters for the nineties

There is something compulsive about a newsletter. It looks interesting and independent, which makes it more likely to be read than a brochure. But there are also drawbacks. A newsletter is expensive and time-consuming. It is difficult to find enough articles, and arranging effective distribution is a problem. Colleagues will deride it, and contributors will fail to provide stories. Many newsletters cease publication after three issues.

A newsletter has a short life (around three months), compared with a brochure which could last three years. So to be cost effective, the newsletter has to be twelve times more effective than a brochure. Few newsletters can meet that criterion, and most newsletters support company brochures rather than competing with them.

To make a newsletter succeed calls for good planning. It is worth setting some guidelines. These will help you organize your newsletter and avoid the many pitfalls that exist.

WHY DO YOU WANT TO PRODUCE IT?
Do you want it to produce extra sales, to gain corporate awareness, to persuade opinion formers, or to keep your staff informed?

You don't have to cram every objective into one newsletter. With today's DTP (desktop publishing) software, it is easy to produce different newsletters for different target markets.

WHAT BUDGET WILL IT HAVE?
Newsletters aren't cheap, and it is important to know in advance how much yours will cost. Your costs will include

the editor and contributors' time, plus all the hidden production costs in transport and secretarial support.

WHO WILL IT BE AIMED AT?

Newsletters need to be carefully targeted. Many companies aim their newsletters at both staff and customers, and this leads to a less interesting newsletter. Customers don't want to read about 'births, deaths and marriages'. So you should either produce one newsletter, aimed at one of these targets, or else two newsletters (one for staff, the other for customers).

Your newsletter must be written at the right level for its readers. Building labourers will need a simple content, while research physicists will need more detailed information. But bear in mind that many readers will not be familiar with your products, and even highly educated people don't want too much information.

WHAT SIZE OR FORMAT WILL IT BE?

Newsletters are usually either A4 or tabloid. A4 is easier to produce using DTP, and it goes more easily through photocopiers. It is also a neat format. On the other hand the broadsheet wins on impact, because its larger pages allow more varied layouts. It also allows more information to be included, though this is not always a good thing.

The newsletter doesn't have to be in full colour, nor printed on glossy paper. Many successful newsletters are simple typed sheets. The simpler the format, the easier it is to produce, but there will be readers who call for a more sophisticated approach. Be alert to this possibility, and judge when the time is right to call for a bigger budget.

HOW MANY PAGES SHOULD IT HAVE?

The number of pages partly depends on how much you have to say. A multi-national company will have no difficulty regularly filling twelve pages of a newsletter, while a small firm will struggle to fill four sides of A4.

It is sensible to start with the smallest number of pages you can confidently fill, bearing in mind that your readers will appreciate conciseness. Few company newsletters need to be more than eight pages.

WHERE WILL THE INFORMATION COME FROM?

You can do it the hard way, and collect all the information yourself. Or you can get help by appointing a contributor in each department or division. These people will be your eyes and ears. The most skilled will be able to write the articles themselves, while others may only be able to supply you with the raw data.

You can motivate people to give you more news by printing their name against the articles they produce (either 'by Sandra Middleton, Maintenance Department', or else 'information from Sandra Middleton'). You can also include their name in the credits box inside the newsletter.

> A leading construction firm sent its staff a note four times a year asking for stories for the newsletter. It rarely got any response. At last it offered £5 book tokens for each main story printed – and received a big number of stories.

HOW WILL IT BE DISTRIBUTED?

For a newsletter aimed outside the company there are several options. The representatives can be asked to distribute them. They will see this as a minor part of their job, and one which doesn't bring immediate sales. So although reps need copies they should not be relied upon as the only means of distribution.

Leaving copies with distributors is like asking reps to deliver them. It is common to come across dusty bundles of old newsletters in wholesalers' warehouses. The wholesaler doesn't see it as his job and isn't motivated to do it.

Direct mail is a costly but effective way of ensuring that the newsletter gets to your customer's desks. You will need to set up a database (if it doesn't already exist) containing readers' names and addresses, and this will need to be regularly updated. If you have a 15 per cent turnover in people, a database with 5,000 names will need 750 changes a year. Remember to include the reception desks, canteens, rest rooms, and other communal and public places.

WHO IS TO HAVE DAY TO DAY CONTROL?

Who should have the final say over contentious material? There won't be disagreements during the newsletter's first issues, but differences of opinion will emerge later. How should a strike be handled? How should a wage round be treated? There needs to be a plan for such eventualities.

HOW OFTEN WILL THE NEWSLETTER APPEAR?

Produce a newsletter too often and you will run out of stories. It is easy to underestimate the effort required to bring out a newsletter regularly. You could start with a single issue and then review its success. Alternatively, you could decide to produce two or three issues a year, and then increase the number if necessary.

You don't have to issue the newsletter at set intervals. Your editions might be timed to coincide with major exhibitions or new product launches.

WHAT WILL BE ITS TITLE?

A title that includes the company name will be popular with the Chairman, but will sound less independent to its readers. On the other hand, a simple newspaper name (such as the *Clarion*), might reduce the newsletter's effectiveness if readers don't connect it with the company.

Below the title you can have the words, 'published by the ABC corporation'. This frees you from having to choose a title with the company's name, while ensuring that the reader knows the newsletter's source.

You can also have a 'statement of purpose'. This defines the objectives of the newsletter, as for example: 'Promoting standards in the electrical component industry'.

Companies often select a title that indicates the nature of the business. The Civil and Public Services Association has a publication called *Red Tape*. Other newsletter titles pun on the idea of communicating: the Food and Drink Federation has one called *Feedback*.

Newsletter titles

Chronicle	Comment	Commentary	Communicator
Correspondent	Courier	Despatch	Diary
Echo	Express	Extra	Focus
Gazette	Globe	Guide	Graphic
Herald	Indicator	Informant	Informer
Inquirer	Insight	Intelligence	Journal
Leader	Mail	Mercury	Messenger
News	Notebook	Observer	Oracle
Post	Probe	Quest	Record
Report	Reporter	Review	Scene
Signal	Source	Standard	Star
Talk	Telegraph	Times	Topic
Update	Voice	World	

DRAWING UP A PLAN

Sometimes all the good stories are crammed into the first issue, so that subsequent issues are disappointing. It helps to draw up an editorial schedule (as in the table below) showing which articles will appear in the first three to four issues.

Staff newsletter first issue: schedule

Page 1	Middle east export story
	Sales appointment
	New trainee scheme
Page 2	Interview with Quality Manager
	Review of new pump product
	Light-hearted look at customers
Page 3	Round up from the regions
	Production quality awards
	Company plan: update
Back page	New technical literature
	Football team results
	Charity bed pull story

Draw up a schedule for future issues, to see where information is needed.

SELECTING STORIES

Use a wide range of stories to keep the newsletter interesting. You will need an average of three to five stories per page. They should be a mix of serious and light-hearted news.

Always put the most important story first. Ensure that the lead story is not one that your readers already know about. This can be a problem if the newsletter is issued at lengthy intervals. If you want to run a story which happened some time before the newsletter was published, find a new angle for the story. A year-end result could be reviewed as 'Where do we go from here', while a story about a major order could be headed 'How the big order was won'.

REGULAR FEATURES

Newsletters benefit from regular features, because they give it consistency and aid branding. Listed below are some examples

Regular features
- 'From the Chairman's office'
- Focus on a different department or region in turn
- 'Round up' from around the country
- New patents
- Appointments, promotions and retirements
- Case study
- Regular features. See 'Topics for a newsletter' below for more story ideas.

CONTENTS

Readers want to read about news. According to research, employees want information in the following order:

1 Organization's plan
2 Personnel policies
3 Productivity improvement
4 Job-related information
5 Job advancement opportunities
6 Effect of external events on job
7 Organization's competitive position
8 News of other departments/divisions

9   How my job fits overall organization
10 How the organization uses profits.

Personal news (about births and birthdays) came as low as seventeenth, while the editor's favourite 'Financial results' came fourteenth.

Employees want to know what direction the company is taking, and how this will affect their jobs. They want real information, and they aren't interested in trivial news.

Topics for a newsletter
Advertising/promotion: What promotion is being carried out? What does it cost? Who is it aimed at? What message is it trying to communicate? What effect does it have?
Analysis: A review of the past ten years' progress, or the success of a product. You can review non-competing products, or even review your competitors' activities.
Annual results: How the results affect the company and jobs.
Applications: Newsworthy ways in which the company's products are being used
Appointments/promotions: What is the person's track record? What factors led to his promotion? What does the new job entail?
Around the regions: How people at distant locations are contributing to the company. What problems do they face?
Awards won: Have the organization or individuals won any awards for training, productivity, export, being a good supplier, or quality?
Better business: Advising customers on accounts, selling or collecting debts. Services available from the organization: marketing advice, technical information. Other sources of information.
Case studies: How the company's skill has helped solved a problem.
Celebrity visits: Has anyone famous visited the organization or performed an opening ceremony?
Charity events: How has the organization or its employees helped charities?
Competitions/winners: Newsletter competitions provide welcome light relief.

Contracts/orders won: Have interesting or prestigious contracts been won? Have difficult contracts been carried out – those which demonstrate technical expertise or the ability to handle large amounts of business?

Crossword: Good crosswords have clues that relate to the industry or company.

Customer orientation: What do customers need? What do they see as the organization's failings? How can service be improved?

Day in the life: What is it like to be an Accounts Supervisor or a Warehouse Operative? What problems do they face? What do they like about the job?

Departmental review: A look at a specific department (e.g. Parks and Leisure or Accounts). What is the function of the department? How it can help other departments. Who's who.

Environment: How do the company's products affect the environment? How is the company helping solve ecological problems?

Exhibition review: What does the exhibition stand look like? What level of interest was there at the last show? How much was sold?

Free gifts: Perhaps a local supplier will give away a limited quantity of his product to the first 10 or 100 readers who send a coupon?

Glossary: Explain what the jargon means, including all those abbreviations whose meaning readers are too embarrassed to ask.

Human interest stories: Births, engagements, marriages, retirements and deaths. Interesting holidays, fund-raising activities or hobbies.

Human achievements: What have individuals achieved, whether in their business or personal lives?

Humorous articles: An ironic look at some aspect of the business.

Interview with an interesting or senior person: What impact does their job have on the company? What issues are they having to handle? What are their plans?

Literature: Describe the range of literature available. At whom is it aimed? What benefits does it offer?

Market analysis: What trends are taking place? How is the company reacting?

Money-off vouchers: Perhaps an organization will allow you to print a money-off voucher? Many leisure or tourist businesses will give a 10 per cent discount to boost sales.

New buildings or factory: What is their function? What did they cost? How will they help the company do better? Will other buildings close?

New products: How do they work? What benefits do they provide? How do they compare with the competition? How are they being launched?

Product evaluation: What does the product do? Who uses it, and why?

Productivity: Measurement of output and costs. How to improve productivity.

Quality: What steps is the company taking to improve quality? Case studies. How the individual can help. How customers benefit.

Reviews: *see* Analysis.

Safety: How to protect yourself. How the company is seeking to reduce accidents.

Sales activity: Are any special sales activities happening? What response has there been?

Sales results: How do sales break down by region, by product or by representative? How do results compare with last quarter or last year? What has caused the variations?

Special offers: Is there a sale or a special deal? For what period? Who is eligible? What qualifications or restrictions exist?

Sponsorship: Who or what is being sponsored, and why?

Systems: How is an order processed, from the moment it arrives to the day the goods are delivered? What records are kept on the central computer, and how is it updated?

Technology: How computerization is affecting different parts of the business. What will happen in the future?

Vacancies: What jobs are available?

Who's who: Putting a face to the name. What jobs different people do.

THE TWO WAYS TO WRITE A NEWS STORY

Stories are usually written in the shape of a triangle which has its base on the ground. You start by giving the reader the briefest of summaries about the story, and gradually enlarge on the various points as the article progresses.

The layout of a news story

Headline ----------------------------->

First sentence -------------------->

Later sentences --------------->

Least important points ->

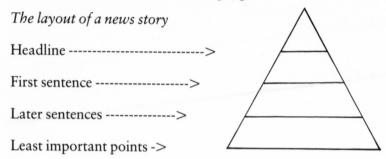

Single Pyramid-shaped story

The headline summarizes the story in less than ten words. For example: 'Warehouse fire costs £50,000'.

The first sentence tells the story as concisely as possible. It should answer the questions, 'who', 'what', 'where', 'why', and 'when'. In this case, our first sentence might run:

> Last month's South Factory warehouse fire will cost the company £50,000 in repairs and lost stock.

As the article progresses down the pyramid, more points are added and the story is fleshed out. At the end of the story are placed the least important points.

There are sound reasons for writing the story this way. Most readers will only read the first fifty words of the article. So if the most important points are at the very start of the article, the reader will grasp the story.

The drawback to this method is that it can be dull and predictable. Which is why some people adopt the second method.

The Double Pyramid method

The Double Pyramid (sometimes called the *Wall Street Journal* method) has a small pyramid on top of a larger one. Instead of starting with the most important point, we get a vignette or case study (usually about a person).

The article might start with Frank Marconi, a farmer in the

American Midwest. It talks about the difficulties he and his family face in making ends meet. As we get absorbed in the life of this individual, we gradually find out why we are reading the article: it is about the international price of cotton.

The Double Pyramid method

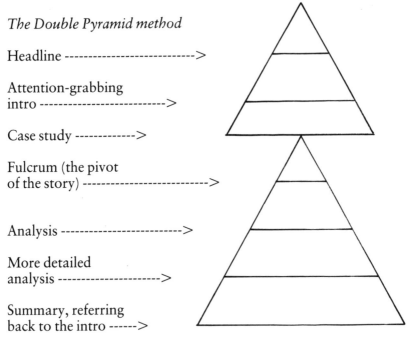

Headline ----------------------------->

Attention-grabbing
intro ----------------------------->

Case study ------------->

Fulcrum (the pivot
of the story) ----------------------------->

Analysis ------------------------->

More detailed
analysis --------------------->

Summary, referring
back to the intro ------>

This method seduces us into learning about a major issue by taking a human angle or by looking at one small aspect of the issue. The Double Pyramid is appropriate for relaxed analytical articles, rather than an urgent page-one story.

How to choose the right style
Use the Single Pyramid method when:
● Your readers are in a hurry
● Your readers will only skim the story
● Your readers aren't very interested in the newsletter
● You are writing a front page news story
● The story is dramatic

Use the Wall Street method when:
- Your readers are happy to read at length
- It doesn't matter if the readers miss the real point of the story
- You are aiming to entertain your readers rather than simply educate them
- You are writing a feature article
- There is no obvious news angle
- The story is not very interesting

ARTICLE LENGTH

Look at a typical popular newspaper – one which is read by millions of people. You will find that the average article is less than 200 words. This could come as a shock to many newsletter editors, whose publications can give 2,000 words to 'The role of tropical hardwood imports in the construction industry'. Lengthy articles are a common mistake among newsletters.

To put it another way, if popular newspapers don't feel their readers will read more than 200 words about sex and murder, it is doubtful whether your readers will get through more than 200 words on a new warehouse.

If you have a long article, you can cut it into several smaller ones. A lengthy article on training could be reduced by putting some of its points into small boxes alongside the main article (see below).

Breaking a large article into manageable pieces

Main article
How training is helping to improve quality

Subsidiary articles
Company policy statement
Training for managers
Training for clerical staff
Case study about an individual
Interview with sales training manager

The smaller articles can be split from the main article by the use of 'box outs', panels below or at the side of the main piece.

GETTING FEEDBACK

Ask your readers for regular feedback. The more you understand your readers, the better the newsletter will be. A 'Letter to the Editor' section is a useful way of achieving this. Encourage people to write in by offering a prize for the best letter. Carry out research to find out what readers think of the newsletter.

HUMOROUS ARTICLES

Humorous articles can look at the lighter side of life in your industry, or they can be totally divorced from work. People with a talent for writing amusing articles are difficult to find, but you could try to find someone by running a competition. With luck, you may find a thwarted writer who has a drawerful of amusing articles. To attract a wide entry, don't restrict the theme.

Humour needs to be controlled. If you value your job, avoid derogatory references to named competitors, the Chairman or the products you make.

COMPETITIONS AND QUIZZES

People enjoy light relief. It helps them while away their lunch break, and gives the Board an intellectual challenge.

You can buy computer programs which create word search puzzles or crosswords. Another favourite is to add an amusing caption to a photograph ('What is Bill saying to Jack?'). You can also add a children's section, which readers can hand to their kids.

Readers like to know who won the prize offered in the last issue. This can be just a couple of lines, or it can be an excuse to interview the winner. You can find out how long he has worked for the company and what job he does.

EDITORIALS

Editorials can be written by the editor, by a specialist guest writer or by a prestigious writer, such as the Chairman or Managing Director. The latter type of editorial is often poorly written, full of platitudes and excessively long. You can solve this problem by getting the Managing Director to agree that his pieces will be a maximum of 200 words in length, and that the Editor will edit the piece as appropriate.

INTERVIEWS

Before you interview anyone, write down a list of questions. Ask yourself what your average reader would like to know. What question is foremost in his mind? What is the most difficult or penetrating question you can ask?

Armed with this information, you will conduct a better interview. It is wise to record the interview with a tape-recorder, having first asked the interviewer for his approval to use the machine, 'so that I don't misquote you'.

After the interview, listen to the tape again, and transcribe the most newsworthy items. By this time, a structure should be forming in your mind. You will be looking for:

- An arresting introduction – something that will make the reader continue reading
- Main topics to be covered in the article

When the article is written, you may want to show it to the interviewee. An independent newspaper can 'publish and be damned', but you may not be in so fortunate a position, especially if the interviewee can fire you.

TEN COMMON NEWSLETTER ERRORS

1   Failure to put editorial on the front page

It is vital to have a lively front cover. Avoid a magazine look with just a single photo on the cover. A newsletter is like a newspaper, and its success depends on its news content. You need to get the recipient reading as soon as he sees the publication.

2   Lack of news stories

Newspapers are weakened by a lack of news stories. Yet often it is only a case of choosing the right 'angle'. A dull feature about the company's activities in South America could be converted into a news story by focusing on a success (such as a newly won contract). If the article can't be made into a news story, try running it as a feature.

Take this start to a front page lead story:

A happy new year to you all! – and what a year it promises to be – for 19XX sees our group on the threshold of a prosperous and exciting era of progress.

This article, which was written by the Chairman, carries on for another 1,500 words with dull statements like, 'Our primary aim must be to maintain and improve the standards we have worked so hard to achieve'. No evidence was quoted to support the idea that an exciting era was about to start. Few employees will have absorbed much information, having been put off by the dull start to the article and its unnecessary length.

3   Weak headlines
A recent newsletter contained the following headlines:

- 100 years of growth
- Ready to face the future
- Building on established strengths

These are platitudes and advertising slogans, not newspaper headlines. The secret of the good headline is to add a fact, a number, a question or the name of an individual. Remember that people are attracted to words like 'new' and 'now'. Avoid abstract words like 'consideration' or 'development'. Include a verb: it makes the headline more forceful. For example, 'Shoe shops' is strengthened when expanded to: 'Four new shoe shops open'.

Headlines should be set in upper and lower case. Capital letters are more difficult because they have no heads or tails to help the eye identify them: each letter has the same shape.

4   Putting a date in the masthead
It is a mistake to put a date on the masthead. Ordinary newspapers have no alternative, but you do. Your newsletter can be used long after it has been published, but once you have added a date, you limit its life.

Including a date makes the timing of the publication less flexible. The date-lined publication must be issued on a specific date, whereas one that is free of dates can be issued at any time without appearing late.

To distinguish between different editions, you can put 'Issue No.' on the masthead, and use a different colour paper or a different colour masthead.

It is also a mistake for the text to refer to 'the forthcoming August shutdown' or to say 'Now that Christmas is over'. This will shorten the life of the newsletter by making it more time specific.

5 Emphasis on the trivial

As we have seen earlier, readers want to know about the company's plans and intentions. They want to learn about the company's successes and about major new appointments.

They don't want pages of information about 'births, deaths and marriages'. This type of information isn't important news because it doesn't affect anyone other than the immediate family. If company politics require that these events be mentioned, they could be listed briefly in a round-up, so that individuals see their names mentioned.

6 Making the newsletter into a company mouthpiece

Owned and funded by the company, the newsletter exists to support company objectives, but it must be seen to be fair and unbiased. In the case of a strike, the newsletter might report the company's offer, and include a quote from the MD as to why the offer should be accepted. It might even run an editorial on the advantages of accepting the offer. But it should avoid being shrill or unduly partisan.

7 Bland writing

Many newsletters are full of dull quotes. Take this real-life example:

> Group Chairman John Mackeson said: 'I am very pleased that our developments in various parts of the country are attracting attention – and such complimentary remarks.

This adds nothing to our store of knowledge – it is an artificial statement created by the Editor. It is very common practice, and this example is patent self-congratulation.

8   Making it too complex

It is easy to make a newsletter complicated, especially when writing about complex matters. Reporting a loss, one company claimed that it had made a profit which had been 'adversely affected by an increase in the requirement for working capital'. The readers were left in the dark by this creative accounting.

In the example below, a computing division is trying to explain a new piece of software. Here is the first sentence from the front-page article:

> A computer-based project management system, which collates and formalizes management information on plans, budgets, costs and resources, is helping BAe to complete projects on time, to specification and within budget.

Midway through the sentence, the reader's brain starts to jam. The main difficulties with the sentence are:

- At 31 words, the sentence is too long.
- The main verb ('is helping') is delayed for twenty words. The reader cannot quickly discover the point of the sentence.
- The subordinate clause 'which collates ... ' is unduly long.
- There are too many abstract ideas in the sentence (system, information, plans, budgets, costs ...).

One solution is to make the sentence shorter and simpler, cutting out many of the abstract words:

> BAe Computing Unit has launched a new program which allows managers to control their projects more easily.

If this sounds a little dry, we could throw away the whole sentence and start again, focusing on reader benefits:

> Is your project running late? Are your costs out of control? If they are, help is at hand with a new piece of software called Promis.

The style will grab the reader's attention, but perhaps it sounds rather like advertising? We could try the Double Pyramid approach:

> Angry and frustrated, Mike Batson looked at his print-outs. 'We're way over cost,' he said. 'Finance Department is going to have our guts for garters.'

Maybe this sounds too dramatic. We could go for a straightforward case history, using the most interesting application:

> The European Fighter Aircraft is now on target, thanks to a new program devised by BAe's Computing Unit.

These four approaches illustrate some important points:

- There are many ways to communicate a story.
- Even the most obscure stories can be told in an interesting way.
- The more complex the product, the more carefully it must be communicated.

SIX WAYS TO MAKE YOUR NEWSLETTER MORE LIVELY
1   Use lots of good photos and illustrations
Good photos enliven a newsletter. When people receive a newsletter, they look first at the photos and their captions. Only then will they turn to the main text.

Photos must illustrate the story. A story about a man who breeds prize-winning dogs must show the man with his dogs. This may sound elementary, but newsletters often use a 'head and shoulders' photo.

If your newsletter is mainly text, find ways of adding photos or illustrations. Aim to have two photos on every page. With today's foolproof cameras, it should be easy for you to take photos of people or events. Keep a loaded camera ready in a drawer, and pack it in your briefcase when you travel. Your own photos will be quite suitable when reproduced across one column, but you will need to commission a professional photographer to take product or installation shots.

There are five main things to photograph:

- The person mentioned in the text (either the subject or the writer)
- The product
- The factory or office
- Installations
- Events

You can also include photos of animals and children if the situation permits – they attract readers.

Photos to avoid

- *Grin and grab*: two people holding a cheque or plaque.
- *Firing squad*: a row of people, usually wearing suits. This type of photo often occurs at conferences or presentations, and the editor feels obliged to show everyone's face. With so many people in the photo, each face is small and no one's personality comes through. It is better to take a close-up of one or two of those present.
- *Station booth mug shot*: a mournful individual staring out of the page with glazed eyes.
- *Gratuitous photos of undressed girls*: the days are gone when it was acceptable to photograph a bikini-clad model leaning against your new range of compressors. Today it would be regarded as sexist.

2 Don't make the layout too crowded

Leave enough space around each story and don't write too much text. Encourage people to read the newsletter by making it accessible.

3 Use a contents box

The contents box should encourage people to read the other pages. So the text should arouse the reader's curiosity, rather than telling him the whole story. Look at newspaper posters. They invariably say: 'Football shock' rather than 'Blackpool wins the cup'.

4 Take advertisements

Advertisements suggest that the newspaper is independent. They also tell the reader that the advertiser values the publication highly enough to advertise in it. The ads also provide a welcome diversion from the editorial which is dedicated to the company that publishes the newsletter.

Even if you don't take ads from outside organizations, you can still run advertisements from other departments within the company.

Your own advertisements
- Recruitment ads from personnel dept
- Suggestion scheme ads
- Request for committee representatives
- Readers' small ads (for sale and wanted)
- Company shop ads
- Company discount scheme ads
- Training scheme ads
- Service departments which offer optional services (e.g. centralized buying, R&D)
- Recruitment ads

These internal advertisements perform a useful task. If you want to improve quality, you can run an ad reminding workers about prizes for reductions in reworking.

5 Use quotes

Almost every story benefits from quotes because they add a human angle, but not every newsletter uses them.

The Patent Office newsletter describes new patents. They range from a new space shuttle to a cat comb which kills fleas – but there are no quotes. Each of the stories could be improved by letting us hear the words of the inventor, who is likely to be one of life's more interesting people.

6 Add fillers

Get in the habit of hoarding unused snippets. They are ideal for filling odd spaces, and they lighten the newsletter.

HOW TO REPORT DULL STORIES

There are some stories that have to be reported, such as the company's financial results. They cannot even be relegated to the inside pages. If the results are good the Chairman will accuse you of treachery; and if they are bad, the staff will think they must be worse than they really are. The secret of handling these stories is to find an interesting angle.

Let's take two common examples of dull news. The first is a new Managing Director. There is no need to say 'The company has appointed a new Managing Director. He is Michael Bland, who is forty-five and has worked in the insurance business for thirty years'.

You must grab the reader's attention in the first sentence. Using the Double Pyramid approach, you could say, 'On Michael Bland's desk sits a plaque with the words 'I'm the boss'. This will lead into a discussion about the man and his characteristics.

A second typical story is the year-end financial results. You could summarize the results in the headline, with 'Profits up 5½ per cent'. If the profits are exactly the same as last year, you could say, 'Profits stable at £1m'. If the business has changed in the last year, you can explain why: 'New pension products boost sales to £155m'.

If profits are down, your headline could be, 'Profits fall 10 per cent'. You could start the article with the explanation 'Lack of demand in the education market caused profits to fall 10 per cent in the last year.' You can also personalize the story. People like reading about other people.

How to add life to a dull story
- A profile (with photo) of the main person mentioned in the article
- Photos or diagrams showing aspects of the story
- Quotations or testimonial (put in a different typeface or colour, or part of the page)
- What this means for an individual
- Reactions from professionals or the press

REPORTING BAD NEWS

Staff like honesty, which is why you should report bad news

without equivocation. If you don't mention the bad news, staff will be less likely to trust the newsletter in future. They will regard it as a company mouthpiece, rather than a real newsletter. By reporting the bad news, you settle rumours and reassure people that redundancies (for example) are not part of a sinister plot to run down the company.

You don't need to include bad news in a sales newsletter. Most readers will not be aware of, or affected by, local issues like redundancies. On the other hand, if you are about to withdraw one of your lines or change prices, you need to tell customers in advance. The newsletter will be a good place to explain why.

THE MAGALOGUE

More companies are introducing editorial features into their brochures and catalogues. This has spawned two new types of media, the magalogue and the brozine.

The magalogue is a cross between a catalogue and a magazine, while the brozine (which we consider later) combines a brochure and magazine.

The magalogue works well for companies that have a wide range of products, and whose customers can be encouraged to try additional ranges. For this reason the magalogue is popular among multiple retailers.

Some magalogues last a full twelve months and provide information about the company's full range. Others are seasonal productions, printed four times a year to coincide with the arrival of seasonal merchandise. But whatever the frequency or scale of the publication, each has the same objectives:

1 To increase sales by introducing the customer to new departments or new products.
2 To create customer loyalty by giving the company certain values such as friendliness, quality or an upmarket life style.
3 To list the products for sale in attractive format.
4 To encourage people to read the publication more thoroughly and retain it.

In producing a magalogue, you are moving from an area you know well – your products and their uses – to the less familiar territory of customers' other interests and activities. So before producing a magalogue, you need to know that your editorial will appeal to them. By commissioning a usage and attitude survey, you will learn about your customers' shopping behaviour, their interests and attitudes. You will need to know about:

- Length: How much detail does the consumer prefer: is it a 100-word *Sun* article or a 2,000-word article in *Harpers*?
- Demographics: How can the reader be classified: for example, is shopping an important and fulfilling role for her, or is it a quick dash around the store after work?
- Topics: What type of subject does she want to read about?
- Aspirations: What does she want to achieve?
- What percentage would pay to buy the magalogue?
- Reading habits: the publications your customers read will be valuable models on which to base the magalogue.

This information will tell you about the style and content of articles to include in the magalogue.

PRICING THE MAGALOGUE

Consider carefully before deciding to charge for the magalogue. It is a useful way of restricting it to people who intend to buy. It can also help you recoup some of the substantial costs. But you may find reader resistance:

A vinyl flooring firm produced a glossy guide to decorating. This magalogue showed people how an attractive floor could contribute to the interior décor. Edited by a professional journalist, the magalogue cost tens of thousands of pounds to produce, and was put on sale at DIY stores around the country at £3.50 a copy.

Hardly any were sold, and they ended up collecting dust in a warehouse. The consumer preferred to get her information from unbiased and less expensive sources, such as glossy home interest magazines.

Articles for a magalogue or brozine
Product categories – related to the company
Human issues and values, relationships
Items of major cost – home, car, holiday, school fees, insurance
Articles about home and family: recipes, child care, pets, home decorating, food, cookery, DIY, furnishing and furniture.
Leisure interests: travel, holidays, hobbies, gardening
Financial: investment, insurance
Health care
'How to' articles
People (celebrities, ordinary people, or people with an interesting job, house or car)
Competitions, quizzes
Advertisements (for example, for shop staff)
Money off vouchers, other sales promotion offers

Magalogue articles are often about things that can't be bought. They come as a positive relief from the pages of merchandise, and they show that the company is not solely interested in profiting from its customers – it is also happy to communicate interesting information.

BROZINES

Most companies have a limited range of products, whose attributes are communicated via a brochure. When the company wants to spice up their brochure with editorial – the result is a brozine.

Brozines are more concerned with promoting a corporate image or extending usage, rather than selling merchandise. They are also concerned with extending the life and usefulness of the brochure, and increasing the frequency with which it is consulted.

Where their products are used by many different people, some companies target a brozine at specific segments (for example, parents or teenage children). Other companies have a club with a regular magazine. Among well-known companies with clubs are Woolworth, British Rail, and W.H. Smith.

The cost of a brozine can be substantially reduced through supplier funding – where the supplier pays for a page on which his products are featured.

6 Write press advertisements that bring business

HOW TO WIN THE READER'S ATTENTION
Your press ad has to work hard to get noticed. It may be surrounded by pages of competing ads. It may be smaller than the rest. It might even be in black and white while others are in colour. Many readers will barely give it a second glance. But you can give it a good start in life by following the best professional practice and drawing up a 'creative brief'.

USE A CREATIVE BRIEF
A creative brief introduces some planning into the advertising process. It stops you writing the wrong ad. And it prevents other people in the company from saying later, 'We should have majored on the colour, not the fabric'. Here are the main points to be covered in the creative brief.

Objectives: What is the ad trying to do? Create awareness, sell more goods, or launch a new service? The best objectives are quantified (for example, 'To achieve 50 per cent prompted awareness among the target market').

Target audience: Who buys your product? Are they 18-30 year old ABC1s (the upper classes and middle classes)? Female owners of small dogs? Engineers in firms employing more than fifty people? Iced bun lovers?
    Here you can add more details about your target market. How much do they know about the product? What do they think of your brand? What is their life style? This information will give you vital clues as to what the ad should say.

Proposition: The proposition is the main benefit you want to convey. A car manufacturer might want to claim that its new model was sporty yet roomy. A beverage might offer a refreshing new taste. A crane might be stronger than its competitors.

It is important to select the right benefit. Don't emphasize 'value for money' if the customer is more concerned with quality. Don't major on a negative:

> An advertisement for a laptop computer claimed that service agents were on hand to mend the machine quickly in the event of a breakdown. This worried readers that the machine would frequently break down.
>
> Not until the end of the ad did the company mention an astonishing selling point: its machine had been voted 'best laptop' by two magazines. That was a powerful proposition that the advertising agency had missed.

Many advertising people use the Unique Selling Proposition, or USP for short. In being 'unique', the proposition must be different from everyone else's. The product doesn't have to be the best: it simply has to be unique in some way. The USP must also be a 'selling' proposition: it must make the consumer want to buy the product.

Some USPs are rational ('Now you can enjoy a pudding without looking like one' (Proposition: the pudding is tasty but not fattening). Others are emotional: 'As the meal ended, the evening began' (Proposition: This liqueur is drunk by upmarket romantic people).

A rational USP comes from the product itself, while an emotional USP is used for a product that has no real advantage over competing brands. The emotional appeal often relies on 'borrowed interest' – something outside the product. Where no advantage exists, you have to look for a positioning that will distinguish the product from all others. In looking for an emotional appeal, you have to think laterally.

Finding the right proposition often involves research. Customers will tell you why they like your product, and what makes it different from your competitors. You may think customers are buying your superior technology, while they are actually buying because your counter staff make them welcome.

Supporting evidence: How can you justify the proposition? Can you quote facts and figures from market research? People need a 'Reason to believe'. Why they should believe a claim that your coffee tastes better? Maybe you have a special way of roasting it? Or perhaps you have experts who select the best beans?

You can provide evidence from market research ('seven out of ten cat owners prefer it'). Or you can mention clinical research from a learned journal. You can quote satisfied customers, or show installations where your product is in place.

Some service companies find it difficult to quantify their benefits; while some products (such as food) have a highly subjective appeal. Yet most businesses can offer proof if they think hard enough.

A southern European island advertised itself as 'One island for four seasons'. The ad claimed that 'Sailing is possible 365 days a year'. But apart from a picture of a beach and a foreign address there was nothing to support these claims.

A sailor would want to know about the extensive mooring facilities, the bustling marinas and the gentle currents. A romantic would like to know about hidden coves, unspoilt beaches and friendly people. Sun seekers would love to hear about the blue seas, golden sands and market stall bargains. Yet the ad mentioned none of these.

Other benefits: Apart from the main proposition, there may be other benefits that the ad should mention in the body copy. By listing them in the creative brief (in order of priority), you can make sure that everyone is agreed in advance about their relative importance.

Tone of voice: If the ad was a person, what manner would it have? Would it be brisk, young and a bit brash? Or would it be cool and efficient? Would it be old, wise and whimsical; or would it be homely and simple?

Media: List the media in which the ad will feature. Each medium is read by a different group of people, so the choice of media determines and dictates the style of the advertisement. An ad designed for *Woman's Weekly* will look different from an ad for *Harpers*.

Constraints: You may not be able to afford large, full-colour ads in expensive publications. This financial constraint will limit how much you can say about your product, and where you should say it. The Code of Advertising Practice is another constraint which may prevent you from making certain claims.

Specimen creative brief

OBJECTIVES
To gain greater awareness of the range of policies offered by MRG plc.

TARGET MARKET
Insurance brokers.

PROPOSITION
MRG supports its brokers by selling only through intermediaries. Therefore MRG is the right company for brokers to use.

SUPPORTING EVIDENCE
Several insurance companies sell their policies direct to the public, and thereby cut out the broker. MRG is committed to selling only through intermediaries.

OTHER BENEFITS
Wide range of policies (motor, household and commercial), low rates, excellent service, national field force, local offices around the country, fast response.

MEDIA
Insurance Age, Brokers' Monthly. Full page colour.

TONE OF VOICE
Assured, sympathetic, dignified.

This creative brief sets out the purpose of the ad and its parameters.

Having agreed *what* you are going to say, the next task is to decide *how* to say it. Every press ad has three main components: the headline, the visual and the body copy. Other components, which we consider later, include the company's name and address, a logo, a strapline and possibly a coupon.

MAKE THE HEADLINE STRONG
The headline has two jobs to do. First, it must attract the reader's attention. Second, it must persuade him to buy your product.

It isn't enough to be strident. Shouting at the reader may attract his attention but it won't convert him. There are two ways to gain the reader's attention. Firstly, the ad needs a big, bold headline. The words must leap off the page and be simple enough for the casual reader to understand. Avoid long, difficult or unnecessary words. Secondly, the headline has to make the reader stop and think.

Headlines that don't work
Dull announcement
Statement of the obvious
Obscure pun
Literary reference
Company or brand name
Irrelevant benefit

Ads have to shock the reader, make him smile or make him think. They should make him curious, tell him something he didn't know, or simply make him want to buy.

Headlines work better when they are on top of a photo or illustration. A headline is better than a photo in communicating a proposition: it is more concise and usually has more stopping power. If the reader doesn't see a headline at the top of the page, he is more likely to turn over.

Professional copywriters create a large number of 'concepts' or rough headlines for every ad they produce. If you haven't drafted at least fifteen concepts, you may have missed a really powerful ad which is just out of reach in your mind. Each concept will trigger another thought, and it may be the fourteenth or thirtieth that is the right one.

Once they have been written, the concepts can be grouped into four to six main headings. This will help you organize your thoughts and reduce the options. Delete concepts that duplicate each other.

If in doubt, use a straightforward headline that tells the story. There is nothing wrong with '15 per cent off all beds now'. Avoid a headline that jokes simply for the sake of it. If it doesn't sell, it's wasted effort.

TIPS FOR BETTER HEADLINES

Make the headline relate to the product. Make the headline relevant and simple. Make the product the hero of the ad.

Beware of headlines that compare your product with something else. A nappy was recently compared with a colander, and a factory with matchsticks. Unless the comparison is immediately obvious, you will lose a percentage of your readers.

Use words that ring bells in the mind: Make a list of words that appeal to your reader. An investment company wrote:

> We venture beyond the capital

Investors simply had to read an ad with such an intriguing headline.

Relate the ad to its context: Knowing how complicated some financial advice can be, a finance company ran an ad in the personal finance pages of a newspaper with the headline:

Confused by all this? You needn't be

The ad correctly forecast that the financial editor's advice would raise as many questions as it answered.

THE VISUAL

Pictures encourage people to read the ad. So whether you are using a photograph or illustration, the visual part of the ad is vital. The visual need to be just as arresting as the headline. Make it big and bold, and get close to the subject.

Don't be embarrassed about producing a rough visual to accompany your words in the early stage of the ad's creation. Most advertising people are quite capable of understanding that a matchstick man with a stick is really an architect with a set of plans.

KEEP BODY COPY TO THE POINT

If your headline and illustration has attracted the reader, he may decide to look at the small print – the body copy. This is where you explain the headline, confirm the facts and add extra selling points.

If you can make people read the body copy, you have a better chance of selling them your product. But because body copy looks boring, few people actually read it. They are satisfied with having broadly understood the ad, and so they turn the page.

Even fewer people read *long* body copy. The exception is where the reader is deeply interested in the product (such as a major purchase, a life-style decision or a leisure interest). So before going into great detail about the technicalities of your loudspeakers, ask yourself whether the reader wants so much information. Take this excerpt from a car ad:

For a limited period, all Peugeot 205 and 309 diesels are available with a £200 Introductory Bonus. It works like this: Claim your Diesel Bonus Voucher by calling the Freephone number below. Then, if you buy and register your new 205 or 309 diesel before 15 December 19XX your dealer will validate the voucher and return it to Peugeot's Head Office. You will then receive a cheque for £200 direct from Peugeot,

so the Bonus will not affect the deal you make with your local
Peugeot dealer – so you are likely to save even more.

This 100-word paragraph makes the deal sound unnecessarily complex. The information could be cut by 60 per cent,
leading to an increase in comprehension:

> You can claim £200 off a new 205 or 309. Just phone
> Freephone Peugeot for your Bonus Voucher. It will save you
> £200 off the cost of a new Peugeot if you buy before 15
> December 19XX.

You can encourage people to read body by breaking it up
with small illustrations. You can also lay out the body copy
in a visually interesting way rather than the usual two
columns.

So how do you write body copy? Imagine you are on a
train, and the person opposite asks about your product.
Write the ad as you would talk to him. Not in pompous
words, nor with unnatural sales excitement, but in a normal
tone of voice. You speak with quiet conviction, listing the
product's benefits and demonstrating how it works.

You can't explain every detail in a press ad. So don't try.
For the sake of clarity and single-mindedness, some
information has to be left out. Keep the ad simple, and leave
some detail to be explained in a brochure.

HOW TO WRITE BETTER BODY COPY
Avoid laborious scene-setting. Take this sentence which
appeared at the start of some body copy:

> The current economic climate has brought increasing pressure
> on many organizations to cut operational costs, creating a
> dilemma over the management of their real estate services.

It is impossible to discover what this ad is selling (property
management, in fact). Consumer products can be just as bad:

> Energy. Boundless in some people. A little less evident in other
> people. All kinds of factors can determine the amount we
> have at any one time. Fulfilment, for example, can act like a
> tireless dynamo.

Had enough? The readers probably have. The ad was for meat, and the lesson is clear: don't meander around your subject: get straight into the sale.

Compare now the economy and speed of this challenging body copy:

> It can take time for a driver to adjust to different road conditions. Conversely, it can take a BMW 0.03 seconds.

Avoid analogies: Take this piece of body copy:

> Today's SCA is no low-technology basic company, surfing on the wave of a booming pulp market.

Probably written in California, this analogy may be clear to young surfers. But to middle-aged UK top businessmen (the target market) it sounds distinctly odd.

Be positive. In the example above, the words about being a 'low-technology company' are burned on to the reader's mind. Every time the company denies it, the words are fixed more strongly. It is better to present positive statements about the product. In this case, SCA could emphasize that it has high-tech products, owns advanced patents or employs hundreds of scientists.

Some ads start with negative statements, which could easily be converted into positive points. Take the jam company that said its marmalade was 'never a bitter experience'. Or the car company that wrote:

> We thought our 16-valve engine was incomparable. Apparently not.

Identify the main points: If you have several distinct benefits to convey, try giving each benefit its own paragraph, like this excerpt from a data firm:

Comprehensive. 25,000 equities, 44,000 bonds, 50,000 economic series, plus futures, forex and interest rates covering over 35 countries.

Timely. On-line direct to your PC for fast, easy access.
Accurate. Our data is collected, validated, and checked by a 120-strong team – using multiple sources to ensure reliability.

PROVIDE A PAY-OFF

Body copy in press ads often finishes with a pun, sometimes known as the pay-off. The copywriter is rewarding the reader for finishing the copy, and making him feel well-disposed towards the company. He is also showing off to other copywriters.

Verbal humour isn't difficult to write, but most puns have been over-used. For any type of business there is a set of idioms. Clichés about cars include:

- Driven up the wall
- Drive you round the bend
- Back seat driver
- Take you up blind alleys
- A one-way street
- Drive like a madman
- Road hogs
- Right up your street

Instead of chewing a pencil for hours on end, you can take a short cut by looking in a dictionary of idioms or a copy of Brewer's *Dictionary*. But use idioms sparingly: many have become clichéd through excessive use.

INCLUDE THE MINOR ELEMENTS

At the bottom of the ad goes your *company name*, the *address* and *telephone number*. If you leave it out you aren't really trying to get sales. If you are selling packaged goods, you will need to include a *pack shot* – a photo of your product. If you can't use a pack shot, your *logo* will provide a visual reminder for the reader.

A *list of stockists* is important if your product has limited or selective distribution. Some ad agencies put the stockists' list on the facing page of the publication. This stops the ad looking untidy.

Other options include *a money-off coupon*, or a *coupon* to be mailed back to you for more information.

ADD A STRAPLINE

A 'strapline' or 'tag line' usually appears underneath the logo. (It is called a slogan by those who aren't in the know and a slogo by the *cognoscenti*.) The strapline summarizes the product's benefits in a memorable way. Put the same strapline at the bottom of the ad, on point-of-sale material and on brochures, and you link all the different promotional elements together.

Writing a strapline is like writing a headline. You sit down and produce fifteen or more short lines (each two to five words long). Try different approaches, and look at the problem through different eyes.

Write down the key words that relate to the industry, and see if there are idioms or sayings that you can capitalize on. Occasionally, a strapline becomes a national saying, but people usually forget which brand it was attached to.

Here are some straplines for a company selling basic cruises in the Turkish Aegean:

- Pure Turkish Delight
- It's plain sailing
- Turkey without the trimmings
- Sail back in time
- The most idyllic holiday ever
- Rule the Aegean for a week
- A charter as old as time
- So good, you'll go overboard

Straplines often make good headlines because they summarize a major benefit in a pithy way. Similarly, discarded headlines often make good straplines, though they may have to be shortened. So when you are halfway through writing an ad, look at the straplines. One of them might make an ideal headline – it could be shorter and wittier than the headline you originally wrote.

How to tell if an ad is on target
Does the headline communicate the proposition from the creative brief?
Does the headline contain a real benefit?
Is the headline easy to understand?
Is the selected benefit the most important one?
Does the ad appeal to your target audience?
Does the ad show your product clearly?
Does the layout allow room for your company's name and address, a strapline and a coupon?
Does the ad avoid talking down to readers? Does it avoid offending them?
Are you sure the ad doesn't over-claim?
Is it honest, decent, legal and truthful?

Agencies often produce ads with such clever headlines and appealing illustrations that the client is captivated into approving it. If you have a nagging doubt, ask yourself these questions.

THINGS TO SELL
Every product contains many benefits. So before you opt for a simple proposition like 'We're cheaper', consider what other benefits might attract a reader. In the list below are just a few. But you must be able to justify the claim. Any product that simply claims to be 'modern' has usually been designed twenty years ago.

Selected list of benefits
Beautiful
Bright
Cheap
Colourful
Comfortable
Comprehensive
Convenient
Co-ordinated
Design, pattern
Durable
Easy to use
Efficient

Environmental
Exciting
Expensive
Flexible
Gentle
Healing
Healthy
Heavy duty
High performance
High quality
Informative
Labour-saving
Light
Local
Modern
Powerful
Quick
Range
Relaxing
Reliable
Safe
Simple
Speedy
Strong
Stylish
Versatile

Each benefit can mean different things. 'Exciting' could mean a thrilling novel, a gripping computer game or a stimulating conference.

For some products, being cheap might refer to the unit price. For others, it might mean you use less, or that it reduces down-time.

You can also turn apparent disadvantages into benefits. Expensive products are desirable because, being costly, they are available only to the rich. Therefore the high price is a benefit. Even ordinary objects can be given this positioning. Stella Artois ('We scour the earth. Then we charge it') is a good example of price being used for dramatic or comic effect.

SELLING COMMODITY PRODUCTS

What about products which have no unique benefit? Take a commodity like a packet of nails, where one company's product is identical to its competitors. Here the ad could emphasize the effective packaging, the reliable delivery, the range of related products, the extended credit terms, the product quality or the friendly service.

It could emphasize a generic benefit which other companies ignore: the nails may be sharp, straight, strong, suitable for many surfaces, free from rust, have a flat head or come in a range of sizes.

> Decades ago, at the dawn of mass-market advertising, a dairy firm told people its milk bottles were 'washed in steam'. This impressive hygiene claim was actually standard industry practice. But no other company had recognized that it could make a strong proposition.

> High street banks offer savings schemes that have special tax advantages. The tax exemption was created by the Chancellor of the Exchequer and is available from any savings institution, but each bank manages to make it look like a proprietary scheme.

WORDS THAT SELL

As we saw in chapter 2, the eye is attracted to 'newsy' words. It can help if your ad uses words like:

New
Now
Limited offer
Sale
Special offer
Free
Guarantee
Cheap
Discount
Reduced
50 per cent off
Win

You
Introducing
Welcome

But beware of using words or themes that cheapen your product. If the ad looks vulgar, people will think your products are down-market or shoddy. Some supermarkets have restrained, even tasteful 'money-off' ads, while other grocers have a 'pile it high, sell it cheap' approach. Even though the products are priced the same in both cases, the effects are completely different.

Numbers, too, have stopping power. Take ads like 'All 3 CDs for only £2.99', or 'Built with 2001 in mind'. But keep dull product codes out of the headline, as in:

Minolta EP8600
A new formula for high speed success

SIXTEEN HIDDEN BENEFITS THAT PEOPLE BUY
Successful ads appeal to a deep-rooted need. Here are the most important ones:

Individuality: People like to feel they are independent. As mass-marketing reduces the difference between objects, people like to be seen as individuals.

Investment: Investment means that a purchase will last a long time or gain in value. This applies not just to financial services or antiques, but anything that shouldn't break down or wear out, whether washing-machines or jumpers.

Money-saving: We all like to get a bargain. We like to be known as canny buyers. Promotional offers, money-off ads, and sale ads all come into this category.

Keeping up with the Jones's: Though rarely expressed in such a blunt fashion, this type of appeal works when subtly done. Many people are inherently competitive.

Toys for the boys: Lots of men are oversized boys. They like machines with knobs and dials. From cars to hi-fi, from lawn mowers to computers, every machine is a potential toy.

Efficiency: Anything that simplifies our busy lives is worth having. That is the appeal of ads which tell us the product is versatile, that it will organize us, or that it will make fewer demands on us.

Association: We have images of ourselves – as country ladies, as squires, as sophisticated business people. We want to resemble our heroes – which is why celebrities often feature in ads.

Elegance, beauty and sophistication: The promise of health, youth or good looks are powerful motivators. Becoming fit or slim also comes into this category.

Novelty: We like new things: purchases we can show our friends. If it's faster, smaller or more powerful, we'll be interested in it.

Altruism: People like to help others, to be worthwhile, and to be seen to be generous. Appeals to charity or generosity can work, especially if they benefit us or free us from guilt.

Display: We like to show off our wealth, whether a faded oriental carpet, or high-tech television or a charming twelve-piece porcelain collectors' set of rustic cottages. These are visible evidence of our affluence.

Status: Power is sought after, while status proves we are wealthy. If a gold card will make people defer to us, we will want it.

Insurance: People want security, stability, and reliability. They want better things for their children or spouses.

Knowledge: We like to buy knowledge because we think it will give us wisdom, charisma or a better job.

Style: Everyone wants to be seen to have good taste. Our clothes, our home furnishings, even our tennis racket needs to be fashionable.

Pampering: After we've improved ourselves, protected our families and shown off to the neighbours, we like to be entertained and cosseted. When life gets stressful, people want to relax and to be self-indulgent. A new bathroom suite, a perfume and prepared food are all in this category.

WAYS TO IMPROVE YOUR AD

1 Give it a subheading. Give your advertisement an introductory subhead if you want to draw attention to a specific market. For example: 'School fees', or 'Music lovers'.

You can also use the subhead to draw attention to a problem that people face. For example: 'Are other people reading your secret documents?' Or: 'Leaky guttering?'

2 Use an editorial format. An editorial format looks less like an ad, and people feel more positive and relaxed when they read it. An editorial-style ad also looks more informative and lively. If done in the style of the magazine in which it appears, it will capture some of the goodwill that people feel towards the publication.

3 Don't write for more than one person. If you say, 'Send orders to … ', you break the illusion of personal conversation.

4 Don't leave out body copy. Many advertisers produce ads that look like posters. They think that it is enough to have an image of a model, a pack shot and a banal headline like 'The subtle difference'.

Record companies, film distributors and publishers believe

that the name of a pop group, film star or author is sufficient to attract sales. Yet all consumers need to know why they should buy the product. Without body copy, the ad is deprived of its sales points, and the product is only bought by loyal fans.

Some drinks, perfumes and clothes companies think that there is nothing to be said about their product. They assume that the photography will make up for the lack of words. Yet all perfumes have distinctively different types of smell, and are positioned to attract a different type of purchaser. Without body copy, the reader will have to guess about the nature of the product.

4   Always include a headline. Recently there have been headless ads for a major bank, a coffee brand, a hair conditioner and a fitted kitchen company. In such cases, the reader is expected to plunge into the body copy (if it exists) to understand the ad.

5   Don't make the headline difficult to understand. A charity ad has a picture of African tribesmen under a headline saying, 'Do they have to be driven to extinction before you share your car?'. This ad combines a rhetorical question and a surreal idea – desert people and the family car. Readers have little time – if you want them to share cars, tell them so simply and directly. Likewise, there is a dog-food headline that defies all attempts to understand it:

> Why nutrition for the average full-grown dog
> should be regarded as a specific need.

How much simpler it would have been to write:

> Is your dog overweight?
> New low-calorie dog food will keep your dog trim

6   Don't use your company name as a headline substitute. The purpose of the headline is to convey a benefit – it is not there to draw attention to your name. Yet many headlines just say 'J. Bloggs'. Using your company name suggests a lack of creative thought, and over-reliance on the strength of a brand name. An advertisement should enhance a brand name, not rely on it.

7 Ask for the order. All the people who reach the end of your ad are receptive to your product. So push them to the next stage. Tell them where they can buy your product. Ask them to ring you, or fill out a coupon, or send some money to you.

8 Beware of ads that mock the reader. A building society told potential home loan borrowers that workmen cheated, were unreliable and provided poor quality work. This type of ad will simply worry its readers.

But, proving that rules are meant to be broken, Whitehead and Partners, a school fees firm, gained extra enquiries with a new ad that portrayed parents as dunces. In this case, the impact of the ad overcame its offensive message.

9 Keep the benefit simple. Be single-minded, and go straight for the most important point. If you want to add other benefits, keep them for the body copy, and only refer to them after you have explained the main benefit. Some ads try to say too many things in the headline, and in so doing they make the ad less dramatic and powerful.

10 Offer a comparison. 'Knocking copy' needs to be used carefully. In naming a competitor you give him a free advertisement. Aggressive ads also risk alienating your customers. On the other hand, comparison ads are a good way to get exposure for a small brand that out-performs the well-established market leader.

11 Tell them a story. Everyone loves to hear a tale. Real-life case histories make great reading, especially if the case tells of a real problem.

12 Give it drama. To engage the reader's attention, you have to involve him. Make your ad stand out by giving it impact. Never write a worthy but dull ad. No matter what the market, every product deserves commitment and emotion in its ad. One way to do this is to give it a human angle – bring real people into your ad.

RETAIL ADVERTISEMENTS

Retailer ads tend to look very similar. The headline says 'Giant sale', or 'Fresh food at lower prices'. This is followed by illustrations of five to ten products, each with its own price tag.

Being price conscious, retailers think customers will buy at the store with the lowest price. While this may have been true twenty years ago, few people today will change stores to save 20p off a bag of sugar or £10 off a washing-machine. It is also dangerous to target your appeal at shoppers who have no loyalty other than to money-off. Customers are motivated by many other factors. For supermarkets, they are swayed by easy car parking and by the display of fresh food.

There is a second explanation for the typical retail ad. Manufacturers pay retailers for advertising their product. In taking the money, the retailer is obliged to mention the brand and show the pack. A few retailers, notably Sainsbury, have broken from tradition by showing fresh produce or their own-label products. But for most stores free advertising is difficult to reject.

If a store adopts the usual strategy of showing products and prices, there are ways of disguising this lack of originality. Some approaches are listed below.

Topics for retail ads
- Product groups: a motorists' shop can group items that clean cars, customize them or provide in-car music.
- Information: a fabric shop could provide helpful advice about making curtains, dressing a window, or duvet weights.
- Quality of the merchandise, its ingredients or packaging.
- Staff expertise or friendliness.
- Improved product features.
- Unusual or exotic products that other stores don't stock.

- Services: a shop might be able to order products for customers, deliver them to the home, or install them.
- Guarantees.
- Themes: foreign countries, Green issues, elections.
- Endorsement by a celebrity or store visit.
- In-store competition.
- A promotion requiring the collection of till receipts or wrappers.
- Seasons: spring, summer, autumn and winter give reasons to promote specific products appropriate to the time of year.
- Special Days: Christmas, Easter, bank holidays, Father's Day, Mother's Day, Pancake Day, return to school, summer holidays.

Check list: Things a store can say about itself, other than 'low price'.

WAYS OF IMPROVING A RETAIL AD

Make a sale look different: Most sales look predictable and old fashioned. They claim to be clearing old stock, introducing special purchases or offering seasonal reductions. Yet a sale ad can achieve greater effect if it has a more creative or dramatic theme. The sale could promote the introduction of a new line, celebrate a new manager or a local event, or result from a refit.

Be specific: If you are showing products, you need to be specific. Tell the reader how much each of the advertised items cost. Include a special bargain or loss-leader to attract people to the store. Encourage the reader to tear out the ad and take it to the store.

Show the saving: The old devices are still the best. Cross out the old price, and insert the new one in a bold type face.

Make it stand out: Make sure your ad is more than just a jumble of products. Do this by using a bold layout, and give it a strong headline that stands out.

Add a coupon: With their scissor-lines and their monetary value, coupons demand to be cut out. Some companies use a coupon simply to involve the audience, rather than expecting redemption. Only a small percentage of coupons are redeemed, but you can affect the response by altering the size of the coupon and its worth.

DIRECT RESPONSE ADS

Some products can be sold 'off the page' – directly from the advertisement. They tend to be products that need little explanation or trial.

Direct response ads have to work harder than ordinary advertisements. The consumer can't check the product before buying it. Nor can she ask a shop assistant, or mull over a brochure. So the advertisement has to answer all her questions and allay all her fears. Direct response ads always look busier. This is partly to answer all the questions, and partly because a busy ad will attract readers – it seems to have a lot to say for itself.

HOW TO GET MORE RESPONSE FROM OFF-THE-PAGE ADS

Make a special offer: Encourage impulse purchase by adding something special. It might be 'Buy three, get one free'. Or it might be a free accessory, container or gadget. Free merchandise is particularly attractive, especially if you are offering an item which carries a well-known name (for example, a pen with a famous logo on it).

Provide a guarantee: Mail order customers need to know you will take the product back if they don't like it. The guarantee gives them peace of mind, and removes one more obstacle to purchase. The guarantee should be prominent and quibble-free.

Use an endorsement: Endorsements show that other people have tried the product and liked it. They are useful for adding new benefits into the copy. And a customer can praise the product in a way that would seem boastful if it came from the manufacturer.

Limit the offer: Experience shows that most orders come within a matter of days of the ad appearing in a daily newspaper. By restricting the offer to orders received within two weeks, you will encourage prompt orders and avoid the loss of sales through inertia.

Organize the coupon: The response device has to be easy to cut out. So put it where it can be most easily torn out. On a right-hand page, this is at the bottom right-hand corner of the page. Use a Freepost address – consumers don't have stamps handy. Code the coupon, so you can judge how many people reply from different publications and different ads.

Put a picture of your brochure in the coupon if you want people to write in for it. This will direct attention to the coupon and make it more interesting. Another way of emphasizing the coupon is to put it in a different colour.

Use a credit card telephone number: If readers have a credit card, they can place an order over the telephone. Make sure that the telephone number is prominent.

HOW TO ADVERTISE A SERVICE

Service companies face a special problem: their activities are intangible. A 'with profits' endowment policy that matures in the year 2035 doesn't offer the instant gratification of a hi-fi or a chocolate bar. The task is even more difficult for middlemen like financial advisers, since their services are not unique. Like a retailer, they are merely selling other companies' products.

In an effort to overcome this problem, companies often resort to imagery. Banks use horses or griffins to communicate their services, while their corporate ads use photos of athletes to suggest co-ordination.

Interest rate percentages are common. These are an appeal to price, showing what good value the investment is. But someone will always offer a better price, so interest rates are rarely enough to make people buy a financial service. Another benefit is needed.

164 WRITING TO SELL

People don't buy savings accounts. They buy security, prudence, or peace of mind. They buy a nest egg or they save for a rainy day. They buy to help a charity, or because the company is environmentally sound. They buy for easy access to a cashpoint machine, for the large number of branches, or the extended opening hours. They buy because the company looks friendly, is upmarket, or because it understands young people.

In short, there are dozens of propositions for a service company, and hundreds of ways to express that proposition in a creative way. The same applies to all other services.

Questions a service company must ask
What service do you want to promote?
What does your service stand for? What values are important to you?
What would you like customers to say about you?
What are customers really buying?
What fears do they have?
In what way are you different from your competitors?
How are your competitors expressing their service?
What benefit does your service offer the customer?
How can you express that benefit in a way that is different from your competitors?
How can you express the benefit in a way that all can understand?

A service company should seek to create a brand. A brand is a consistent collection of values, often built up over many years. People buy brands rather than companies or products. Customers trust a brand because it matches their mood or aspirations. For a service company, the branding would manifest itself in the letterhead, logo, and tone of voice used in ads and literature.

Another solution is to promote *products*. Service companies are increasingly branding their services as products, whether a Mexican burger at a fast food restaurant, or a banking service for 18-25 year olds. The more tangible the product, the easier it is to advertise. Unit trusts are a good example. They allow the advertiser to move the discussion away from price, towards ethics, growth opportunities or safety of investment.

Claims a service company can make
1   Consistent
2   Reliable
3   Endorsement
4   Long standing
5   After sales service
6   Friendly staff
7   Experienced
8   Range of services
9   Substantial
10 Conveniently located
11 Well connected, on-line to major organizations
12 Big company experience
13 Ideal for women, ethnic minorities, dog owners, veteran car drivers (niche market appeal)
14 Free information
15 Informal
16 Prestigious
17 Guarantees
18 Your business handled by partners
19 Understanding local needs
20 Small enough to care
21 Specialist skills
22 Unusual departments (e.g. researchers, planners)
23 Unusual service or product (e.g. monthly review)
24 High tech
25 Young staff
26 Socially concerned/green
27 Simple to use, easy to understand
28 Personalized to meet your needs
29 Sales promotion benefits (get fifteen months for the price of twelve, get a free card holder, or win a trip to Disneyland)
30 Thorough, good quality control, everything checked
31 Courteous, old-fashioned service
32 Money saving through expertise
33 Sociable

Check list: all service companies can make a claim about themselves.

BUSINESS TO BUSINESS

Try to make sense of this gobbledegook:

> The highest level intelligent programming environment today. Multi-paradigm support for: frames and object orientation, rule-based logic programming, dynamic hypertext, inexact reasoning and visual dialogue creation, as well as links to traditional programming languages.

This passage consists entirely of product features, without a benefit in sight. But it needn't be so. When you buy a car, you buy an image of power, styling, convenience, economy or luxury; and the manufacturers give you reasons to believe the image. They focus on real benefits, like smoothness and fuel-efficiency. Similarly, business-to-business organizations must talk about the benefits of their product, not its features.

Don't assume your reader knows as much about your product as you do. Don't imagine that he is interested in the technicalities. And don't presume that your product is his prime area of responsibility.

For any business-to-business organization, some benefits are derived from the product itself, and others are extrinsic benefits which stem from the service provided. In the table below, we list some of these benefits.

Benefits for business-to-business advertisements
After sales service
Complete package
Construction strength
Delivery
Flexibility
Free trial
Guarantee
Installation
Insurance
Interest free credit

Leasing
Maintenance
Quality control
Quantity sold
Price
Range of products
Reliability
Research findings
Rugged
Sales to well-known organizations
Simplicity
Size of company
Training
Upgrade facility
Well-known brand name

Check list: What exactly does your product offer a company?

Many business-to-business products have common benefits. Computers offer faster processing or a networking facility. Disks offer reliability. Software offers database, program writing, or word processing. Few products maintain a competitive advantage for long. So you need to analyse exactly what your customers are buying, if you want to produce ads that offer more than standard industry benefits.

HINTS FOR BETTER BUSINESS TO BUSINESS ADS

Avoid cluttered ads. Some ads are so fussy that there is nowhere for the eye to rest. In others the headline is no larger than the body copy. A recent full page ad contained 5 headlines, 7 logos, 3 phone numbers, and 21 'bullet points'. Because of the clutter, readers were left uncertain as to what the ad was actually selling.

Be careful about negative ads. One ad was headlined 'Hidden extras'. It aimed to tell the reader that the product had more functions than its competitors. But readers took the ad at face value – and worried about hidden extra costs.

Include any quality marks such as BS5750, BBA, kitemark, or membership of trade associations. They are a strong selling tool.

Make it lively: Business ads needn't be dull: there is a place for amusing or challenging ads. Business people are ordinary human beings who like to be entertained or wooed. Your ad needs to stand out; cartoons, unusual photos or a different proposition can help you achieve that. Weigh up the staid offering of your competitors, and ask yourself whether your ads could stand out more clearly.

RECRUITMENT ADVERTISEMENTS
Job hunters have simple needs, which is why most recruitment advertisements are so straightforward. Job hunters want to know about three things:

THE JOB
Its title
Its salary
Its fringe benefits
Its reporting structure

THE COMPANY
Its location
Its name
Its industry

THE CANDIDATE
Qualifications and experience required
Age range
How and where to apply

Recruitment ads are crowded on the page, so job hunters scan the page looking for key words – particularly a job title. As a result, most job ads end up looking very basic, in order to gain visibility on the page. Below is a typical example.

Automotive Components
ENGINEERING MANAGER
West Midlands   £25,000 + Car
A multi-national manufacturer of automotive equipment, this

European-based group has through growth and acquisition doubled its sales since 1987 to their present level in excess of £2bn.

This division's activities are focused upon car and truck underbonnet engine cooling systems. With manufacturing centres of excellence already established in strategic locations, this exciting new venture will lead the engineering team through all future UK model engineering development programmes..

Reporting to the general manager, your brief will involve developing the design engineering resource in support of on going sales development programmes across the UK based vehicle OEMs.

The presence and maturity required for this position suggests that applications will be aged 30-40 and already holding a senior engineering position allied to automotive systems engineering development.

Probably qualified to degree level, you will have developed excellent interpersonal/communication skills and experience of modern CAD systems. A second European language is desirable.

A straightforward recruitment ad. Would you accept it?

The ad correctly includes all the main points: job title, the money, the company, and its location. It has left out the company's name, because it doesn't want its own staff or competitors to know that it is recruiting. But it has provided enough information to encourage applicants to apply.

A certain amount of jargon is acceptable here (for example, 'OEMs' and 'underbonnet systems'). If you can't understand these words, you don't deserve the job.

But other jargon simply results from slack or pompous writing. Take the tortuous third paragraph. This is full of unnecessary abstract words like 'resource', and contains errors of grammar (It is the person, not the brief, who reports to the General Manager). The whole ad could be rewritten more simply.

Automotive Components
ENGINEERING MANAGER
West Midlands   £25,000 + Car
The company is part of a leading European multinational

business which makes automotive equipment. Since 1987 its sales have doubled to £2bn.

The division is Europe's largest manufacturer of vehicle cooling systems, and its exciting new design programme will develop new products for UK vehicles.

Reporting to the General Manager, you will boost the company's design engineering skills, and help to increase sales to vehicle OEMs in the UK.

You probably possess a degree, and are aged 30-40. You currently hold a senior engineering position in the automotive or similar industry. You can communicate effectively with other people, and you are experienced in CAD. A second European language is desirable. Please write in strict confidence with full details of age, qualifications and earnings to:

This revised ad is shorter and easier to understand.

HOW TO BOOST THE QUALITY OF RESPONSE FROM A
RECRUITMENT AD
Don't demand irrelevant attributes: Decide which aspects of the job are vital, and those which are desirable. It is tempting to ask for added skills, such as languages or educational attainment. But you could end up with a complex ad, and a job so demanding that no one is qualified for it.

Add your logo, an illustration of your product, or a picture of the job environment (for example a sales rep and his car), to make the ad stand out.

Make the job sound interesting. Describe the challenges, the independence and the scope.

Reassure applicants. If you are using an agency, tell applicants their application will not be forwarded to any company they specify. This means that the employees need not fear his own company will discover that he is seeking a new job.

Keep the headline simple: Beware of obscure headlines which people can't understand. This strange ad was for a computing job in Helsinki (perhaps it sounded better in Finnish):

Software Engineers
Room for improvement? Surely not

Beware general headlines which no one will notice, such as: 'The management challenge in a specialist operation' (this was for a Post Office Security Manager).

However, there *is* scope for creative headlines, particularly in specialized publications. A police PRO job could be headlined, 'The police are after you', or 'Wanted', or 'Help police with their enquiries'.

Avoid redundant headlines: In accountants and surveyors magazines, many job ads carry the irrelevant headline 'Accountant' or 'Surveyor'.

WRITING SUCCESSFUL SMALL ADS

Small ads are found in every publication, from *Yellow Pages* to the classified ads in the local press.

The rules about advertising apply just as much to small ads as they do for their bigger cousins. Your ad has to get the reader's attention, provide a benefit, and get a response.

Because of its size, the small ad poses a challenge. How do you squeeze all the information into such a small space? The answer is: you don't. With small ads, you have to be highly selective about what you include.

HINTS FOR A BETTER SMALL AD
Allow enough 'white space' – blank paper around the edges of the ad. That attracts the eye because it looks easy to read. It also ensures that the reader isn't put off by dense type.

Use a picture. This is an important way of gaining the reader's attention. Look in *Yellow Pages* and see which ads catch your eye.

Don't simply list your products. Lists are boring. If you have an extensive range of products, summarize them or indicate that you offer a complete service. Give the reader reasons to use you, rather than the company in the next ad. Do this by communicating advantages not products.

Convey the benefit in the headline. It is better to say 'Comfortable retirement home' rather than 'Kingsmead House'. It is better to say 'Musical cuckoo clocks' rather than 'Black Forest reproductions'.

Concentrate on the most interesting part of your product range. Avoid making broad claims such as 'Antique and specialist reproduction furniture for all rooms for the house and office'. It is more effective to promote a waxed pine desk or an oak bookcase. Finish this with a short sentence indicating the breadth of your stock: 'Part of our complete range of beautiful antique and reproduction furniture'.

Don't add unnecessary information such as 'Prop: A. Weston' (Unless A. Weston is world famous). Nor will there be room for a coupon.

GETTING MORE RESPONSE FROM A SMALL AD
With small ads you can either:
- Sell directly from the page, or
- Invite readers to send for more information

The route you take depends on the complexity of your product. Simple products can be sold directly from the page. But more complex products require further stages in the sales process (either a visit by a rep or a catalogue sent).

If you simply want people to ask for a brochure, you can leave out your address, and emphasize the telephone number. This will save several lines of text.

If you want people to send you an order and a cheque, remember to include all the necessary information:
- Illustration of the product.
- Product benefits.
- Size, performance, construction details.
- Price including VAT.
- Your address. Keep it short and don't add unnecessary lines. Don't include both the name of the building and the street number (except for reasons of style). Remember to

include a code to identify which publication provided the enquiry.

- Your telephone number (for queries).
- Payment: whom should cheques be made payable to? You can leave this out providing the name is obvious. Keep the company name simple and put it in a prominent size. Use only one form of the company name (Don't call it 'Lab 16' in the headline and 'AJ Industries trading as Lab Sixteen (Handsworth) Ltd' in the address line).
- Ask for a stamped addressed envelope if appropriate.

7   How to write posters, TV and radio commercials in the bath

People wake to the sound of the radio. They listen while they are washing, dressing and having breakfast. They listen in their cars, at work and when doing housework.

This makes commercial radio good at reaching certain targets. They include housewives, business people, drivers and people who work in factories.

Radio is local. Its listeners are attuned to local shops and events. It should be equally good for selling breakfast cereals, recruiting staff and announcing new cars. But local radio has been slow to gain advertisers' approval.

Part of the problem is the advertisers who will share the commercial breaks with you. Many of the commercials feature loud, enthusiastic voices, getting excited about a furnisher's sale or a new car.

Radio commercials are no worse than the ads that appear in a local newspaper, but the added dimension of sound makes them seem harsher and more strident. So it is not surprising that national advertisers have stayed away from local radio.

For many listeners, the radio is musical wallpaper. They hear it, but they don't listen to it. So before you commit large sums of money to radio, test its effectiveness. Radio doesn't work for everyone.

HOW TO WRITE A RADIO COMMERCIAL

Radio commercials work like any other type of advertisement. You attract the listener's attention, create desire, and get him to act.

But unlike press ads, which are a straight message from the advertiser to the reader, radio can create a whole new world. You can set your scene in the North Pole, in Australia or in the fifteenth century. You can take people forwards in time, or put them in the middle of a raging gale. Few people take advantage of this stunning opportunity. It's like being told by a Hollywood mogul that money is no object. You can have any set and any costumes you want.

Imagine you want to promote the fact that a Scottish store is open on Sunday. The usual commercial would go like this:

Script

Client:	SuperStore DIY, Inverness branch
Title:	Standard
Length:	20 seconds

| Male voice-over (MVO): | Great news for DIYers! Yes, SuperStore DIY is open all day Sunday. There's everything you need for the home and garden – all under one roof. We've paint and wallpaper, tools and tiles, plus the biggest selection of timber, too. We're open on Sunday from 9 a.m. to 8 p.m. So don't miss out. Come along to SuperStore DIY, Inverness, this Sunday – you're in for a great deal. |

Add background rock music, and you have a radio commercial that is the same as all the rest. So let's try another style.

Script

Client:	SuperStore DIY, Inverness branch
Title:	Pub
Length:	20 seconds

Ian:	See you down the pub on Sunday, Andrew?
Andrew:	No, I can't, Ian. I've got to tile the bathroom.
Ian:	On a Sunday!
Andrew:	Yes. Pam's found out that SuperStore DIY is open all day Sunday.
Ian:	That's a shame. I just tell my wife it's shut.

Ian's wife:	Not any more you don't, Ian.
Voice Over:	SuperStore DIY, Glasgow. Open till 8 p.m. each weekday, and all day Sunday until 6. Sorry about that, Ian.

This commercial has real people and a real plot. Inside twenty seconds, we get a glimpse into the lives of Andrew, Ian and his wife. It may not be Jeffrey Archer, but it's the sort of commercial that works well on radio.

Radio, they say, has the best pictures. It lets people create images in their mind. And remember that reading a script is never as dramatic as hearing voices on the air.

Take another example. Imagine it's Christmas time, and you're selling new houses. You want house-hunters to visit your show home and you're holding an open day with mulled wine and mince pies. A conventional radio commercial might go like this:

Script

Client:	Homely Homes
Title:	Standard
Length:	20 seconds

MVO:	If you're looking for a great new home, just come along to the new Badger's Lair development at Cardiff this Sunday. Homely Homes are holding an open day, and there's refreshments for all the family, including mulled wine and mince pies. We're open from 11 a.m. to 5 p.m., so if you're looking to move house, come along to Homely Homes this Sunday.

It puts the message over, but it's uninspiring. Try a more creative approach:

Script

Client:	Homely Homes
Title:	Mulled Wine
Length:	30 seconds

SFX:	Noise of party. Clink of glasses.
Salesman:	Another glass of mulled wine?
Frank:	Er ... no, I'd better not.
Salesman:	Another mince pie, perhaps ... ?
Frank:	(Hesitant) Ooh, well ...

Party noises fade down

| MVO: | At Cardiff this Sunday, Homely Homes are holding an open day at their Badger's Lair development. There's free refreshments for all the family, and you can look around the spacious 2-, 3-, and 4-bed showhomes. |

Party noises fade up again

Frank:	(Decisively) All right, I'll take it.
Salesman:	(Can't believe his luck) You want the house?
Frank:	No, just another mince pie.
MVO:	Mulled wine and mince pies at Homely Homes Badger's Lair Development, Cardiff. We're open from 11 a.m. to 5 p.m. this Sunday.

This commercial isn't expensive to make. In production terms, it is deceptively simple. It takes one hour of studio time, requires three out-of-work actors, a producer and a recording engineer, plus some pre-recorded party noises. And it is a lot more effective than the ordinary single-voice commercial.

'Straight' radio commercials are often appropriate. There are times when people only want to know *what* is happening, *where* it is taking place, and *when*. This applies to specialist audiences for whom every detail is important. It also applies when the message is complicated. If you are advertising a camping exhibition, you will need to tell people:

- The name of the exhibition
- What is new for visitors to see
- What competitions are being held, and what prizes
- Who is exhibiting
- Which celebrity will be present
- The dates
- The opening times
- The location, and how to get to it

For general audiences, it is better to cajole them into action rather than browbeating them. So many radio commercials use the single, over-enthusiastic voice of the local disc jockey, that adding one extra voice and a plot can help your commercial stand out. It also makes your product sound rather more classy than the 'come and get it' style of commercial.

HUMOUR
Humour is a dangerous weapon. What seems hilarious to you may leave someone else unmoved, and what was amusing the first time round will be repetitive on the twentieth hearing. That is why humour should form only part of any radio commercial. The rest of the commercial should be taken up with sales information and character development. The humour should be humour of character, rather than slapstick.

JINGLES
Without a jingle, a radio commercial can sound spare or thin. Most advertisers use a jingle to lull their listeners into a sense of well-being or euphoria. And there lies part of the problem. The smooth relaxing jingle is in danger of making people tap their feet and hum the tune, but it doesn't motivate people to buy.

If you want to create a mood, a jingle will help you achieve that. But listeners are inclined to treat the jingle as just another record they can whistle along to, without understanding what the words are about. People rarely listen to the lyrics of a record: they simply listen to the tune.

Many jingles are difficult to hear. The average listener is chatting to their neighbour, vacuuming the room, or listening in the car with the window down. So clarity is vital. Yet in the jingle, the words are stretched and distorted to match the rhythm, and the instruments are often louder than the voices. The words are often inaudible.

So before opting for a jingle, ask yourself: will it sell my product? Don't be charmed by hearing the exciting beat. Listen to the jingle in 'normal' conditions (at low volume in a traffic jam with the windows down). Above all, keep the jingle within bounds. Don't let it take over the whole commercial.

MISTAKES TO AVOID IN RADIO

1   Failing to include the 'call to action'
Radio messages disappear quickly into the ether, so the sales
message must be the last words the listeners hear. A good
radio commercial leaves the listener with the company's
name or the date of the sale.

2   Cramming in too much information
When a radio voice speaks rapidly, it is because the
scriptwriter has included too many points. Be prepared to cut
out part of the message. It will make the commercial clearer,
and listeners will find it less wearing.

3   Lack of an 'angle'
It's important to choose an angle that distinguishes you from
other advertisers. Don't simply say you install central heating
from £2,750. Why not set the commercial in a freezing cold
house? Why not have a discussion between your salesman
and a suspicious prospect? Or why not have two installers
chatting to each other as they fit central heating? Each of
these scenarios allows you to put over sales points in a lively
way.

WRITING FOR TV

TV may seem daunting, but if you can write a radio
commercial you can write for television. Writing TV has in
the past been the preserve of big spenders, but there is no
reason why it should be. Today many agencies are capable of
producing low-budget commercials, and their number is
likely to grow.

   This chapter helps you understand the world of television
commercials. It will help you write your own TV commercial,
or help you commission one from an agency.

STRENGTHS AND WEAKNESSES OF TV
Television reaches huge audiences. It offers colour, sound,
movement and drama in a way that no other medium can
match. It is also great at demonstrating products.

But the message is fleeting. The commercials that follow yours will get the reader's attention, and your message will be quickly forgotten. The commercial can't be retained for future reference like a press ad, nor pinned on a wall. TV cannot communicate a lot of details, and it is very expensive.

THE COST OF TV COMMERCIALS

TV is full of very slick commercials. So if you have any doubts about matching their quality, stay away from this medium. A recent beer commercial cost £500,000 to make, and the airtime cost £3 million. That is outside most advertisers' budgets. But not every TV commercial costs this amount. Video equipment has fallen in price, computers have grown in power, and more TV channels are becoming available. So the opportunity for smaller advertisers to get on TV has never been greater.

Several factors boost the cost of making a commercial. They include:

- A large cast
- A set that recreates fourth-century Egypt
- A distant location (even half a day's travel for five people mounts up)
- A celebrity
- A big-budget advertising agency
- A well-known film director

The cost of the airtime is affected by:
- The number of stations on which the commercial is shown. Few companies can afford national TV advertising, but many can afford at least their local station.
- When your commercial is shown. Buying fixed spots during the *News at Ten* will be very expensive. Buying a daytime package will be cheaper.
- What discounts you can get. If you are a first-time user of TV, a local advertiser, or you're running a test market, you can get substantial discounts.
- The type of audience you are aiming at. Heavy-ITV viewers (people who watch a lot of ITV) need to see the commercial many times before it registers. Light-ITV

viewers are never in front of the screen long enough to watch your message.

PREPARING TO WRITE
The preparation for writing a commercial is exactly the same as for writing any other advertisement. You need a creative brief that sets out the purpose of the commercial, the proposition, supporting evidence and tone of voice.

You should immerse yourself in the product. You need to know how people use it, where they buy it and what they think of it. Much of the information about the brand will be contained in a detailed marketing plan, but you can often get a better insight by talking to a few shoppers.

You need to know what the competitors are doing. Tearsheets (copies of press advertisements) and videos of TV commercials can be obtained from monitoring firms listed in the *Advertisers' Annual*. Many products in the same market are relatively similar, so it is important to produce a commercial that is different from anything else on air.

There are numerous ways of producing ideas for commercials. Brainstorming, for example, will produce a wide range of ideas. Take a bakery that wants to advertise its pies. Here are a dozen different concepts:

- Natural ingredients (appeal to nutritionally aware housewife)
- Delicious (appetite appeal)
- Good for them (appeal to Mum)
- Ideal for the family (family life style)
- Hot and tasty after a busy day (family life style)
- Traditional fare (old-fashioned values)
- A new food surprise (broaden the housewife's options)
- A new taste (gourmet appeal)
- Secret recipe (mystery appeal)
- Quick to prepare (appeal to convenience cooks)
- A treat for the family (appetite appeal)
- Taste of the country (rural images)

Not every concept will be equally practical. If the commercial requires a Superman character to fly to a supermarket, you will need special effects, technicians and perhaps royalty payments for the use of the character. All of these will greatly increase the cost.

HOW LONG SHOULD IT BE?

TV commercials are generally thirty seconds, but you can also buy twenty-, fifteen-, and ten-second commercials. The last two are generally used as 'cut downs', short versions of a larger commercial, designed to boost frequency of showing. The shorter the commercial, the more times you can screen it, but the less impact it makes. Too short a commercial looks cheap. A major TV advertiser may take forty seconds to make their point, and two-minute spectaculars have been known.

Some TV commercials are word-led. These commercials have extensive dialogue and the pictures play a supporting role. Other TV commercials are primarily visual exercises: their sound track is reduced to a jingle and a voice-over.

The difference lies in the products themselves. A new bank account needs a lot of explaining. How does it work? Do you get a cheque guarantee card? Who is eligible? The words are crucial in this type of commercial.

But if the product is well known, if it can't easily be distinguished from its competitors, and if the benefits are mainly to do with colour, shape or taste, the commercial will rely on the pictures and music.

In other words, products that appeal to the head are word-led, while those that appeal to the heart are more visually oriented.

LAYING OUT A COMMERCIAL

A TV concept is usually shown on a storyboard. This is a piece of card showing rows of TV screens which reveal the commercial in picture-book style. The main images are drawn on to the blank screens, and the script goes underneath. You can make your own storyboards on A2 card, and they are even available in personal organizer form.

The storyboard idea isn't the best way of describing a TV commercial. It is a static representation of a medium which has movement, and that is why some people turn to other methods. Some agencies prefer to act out their commercials, while others prefer a detailed text which describes the emotions of the characters and the setting of the action. Other agencies use an animatic. This is a video of the storyboard, with actors or agency staff doing a rough voice-over.

UNDERSTANDING THE JARGON
It helps to know what the various words of jargon mean. New copywriters often spatter their scripts with technical abbreviations like MCU. More experienced writers concentrate on the script itself. You don't have to include many directions for the shot – the production company can add this kind of detail later.

Types of film
Live Action: Using real people.
Animation: Everything that isn't live action (for example, cartoons, sequence of slides or computer graphics).

Photography
WA: Wide angle shot, sets the scene.
MS: Medium shot, can show two people together.
MCU: Medium close-up.
CU: Close-up, shows a face or a bowl of cereal.
ECU: Extreme close-up, shows a detail (the lips, for example).

Sound
DV: Direct voice, comes from a character on stage.
FVO: Female voice-over. Less rarely heard than an MVO (q.v.).
MVO: Male voice-over: an unseen voice.
SFX: Sound effects. For example, explosions or music.

Camera movement
Zoom: The camera closes in on a subject or pulls back from it.
Pan: The camera swings on its tripod from one

subject to another (For example it might pan from the pack on the shelf to the family at the table).

Tilt: The same as a pan, except the camera moves up or down.

Tracking: The camera physically moves. For this it is often mounted on rails or a car. Tracking can be used to keep up with a galloping horse or a running man, and during the course of the tracking the camera can pan or tilt to take in a new subject.

Changing focus is another way of creating change. The focus can move from a close-up of flowers to a medium shot of a car.

Scene-changing

Mix: Used to be called a dissolve, with one image fading into another. A dissolve can imply that time has passed or the location has changed.

Cut: Change abruptly from one scene to another. A cut is more common in TV commercials because it is more immediate and doesn't waste vital seconds.

Super: Superimpose. A pack is often supered on to the existing scene.

WRITING A SIMPLE COMMERCIAL

Let's take the simplest possible commercial. Imagine you are a fashion retailer, with three shops in neighbouring towns. You want to show the ranges, emphasize the low prices, and tell people about your location. Let's try a simple commercial:

Script

Title: TV reporter
Length: 30 seconds
Video   Audio

An elegant female news reporter is standing outside shop with a microphone.	(In professional TV news style.) I'm standing outside Jane's Fashions in Market Street Chesterfield, and from the window it looks like they've got some bargains. Let's have a look inside.
Cut to: inside shop as reporter rummages.	(2 seconds silence.) Well, it's true, there are some super bargains here.
Holds up jersey.	I love this jersey – it's only £15.99 in the sale. And these dresses are only £7.99. (Voice becomes more enthusiastic, less professional.)
Disappears towards back of shop, puts down microphone, forgets camera.	And look what's over here. (Talking to herself.) Oh isn't this super … Oh I don't believe it (holds clothes against herself.)
End title: Jane's fashions. Addresses.	FVO: Jane's. Where the focus is on fashion.

Here the suave TV reporter does the unthinkable: she loses control, forgets herself. The commercial says 'Our clothes are stunning'; but it isn't the only route. Here are a few more ideas:

- Pop video
- Endorsement by famous actress
- Endorsement by famous local resident
- High-tech effects commercial

- Cat walk commercial ('Here comes Jackie wearing a beautiful number by Gaggia')
- Jane fronts the commercial herself ('I've just picked up some super clothes from Paris, at astonishing low prices.')
- Mood commercial (models on a misty hilltop)
- Disco commercial – lots of flashing lights
- Commercial shot in a stately home
- Life-style commercial – clothes for different occasions, from office wear to evening dress
- Endorsement by old age pensioner (humorous approach)
- Models walking past well-known local landmarks
- Customers talk about why they shop at Jane's

SOUND

Music binds the commercial together and gives the viewer extra information. It tells him that the product is romantic, fun or young. There are several sources of *background music*. The simplest is to use a music library which will have every type of music you could want. Alternatively, you can commission an artiste to create new music. You can also take a well-known piece of music, and either pay a record company to use the original version, or pay for it to be re-recorded. In all these cases, the use of copyright and payment of royalties has to be sorted out.

The *jingle* can help people remember a product, but as a selling tool it is inferior to the spoken voice. Use it to convey a name and an image; but don't try to explain the fourteen benefits of a washing-machine.

You may also need a *voice-over*, which could be anything from a strong regional accent to a standard BBC voice. It is simpler to choose a voice that is acceptable to everyone, but too bland a voice can make the commercial easily forgettable. For the voice-over you can have either an unknown voice or a celebrity. A celebrity who is recognizable by his voice will implicitly be endorsing the product. There will be a difference in price, but many actors cost less than you might expect, especially if they are happy to do this type of work.

You may also need *sound effects*, such as falling rain or thunder. Pre-recorded sound effects are widely available.

TIPS FOR A BETTER COMMERCIAL

1   Make it natural. People don't talk formally or stiffly in real life. Watch a soap opera or a quality TV commercial, and you won't find perfect English. In its place are meaningful pauses and incomplete sentences. A lot of information is conveyed by body language.

2   Don't take the full thirty seconds. Leave enough time for the director to add some meaningful pauses or set the scene. Allow a few seconds for the product name to stay on the screen at the end, and allow a little extra time so that the actors and actresses don't have to gabble their lines.

3   Adopt a different positioning. Look at what other advertisers are saying about themselves, and find something different to say. Position your product away from your competitors. Find something different to say about it.

If you sell double glazing and your competitors are selling low price or a wide range, you could talk about safety, quick installation, guarantees, a case study, quality or a long established business. If your competitor's commercial features the Managing Director, you can hand the words to a housewife, a cartoon character or a celebrity.

Commercials don't have to be set in the here and now. They can be set in the 1920s or the seventeenth century. They can be set in a tropical island, in Poland or in heaven. It is important to break out of self-imposed creative restrictions, providing the location doesn't overwhelm the sales points.

4   Make it smooth. The commercial must flow evenly from one thought to the next, helping the viewer understand the points you are making. Avoid trying to make too many points. It is better to select one important benefit and concentrate on that to the exclusion of everything else. This makes the commercial more cohesive and easier to understand.

5   Develop your characters and locations. Good characters and scenes are fully developed – at least in the minds of the writer, actors and producer. So if your script has two people, don't call them 'Man 1' and 'Man 2'. Give them names. Describe who they are. Write about their aims, how they feel about each other, and what sort of houses they live in. Describe the scene fully. What time of day is it? What sort of day are the characters having?

6 Understand your audience. Children absorb more information than adults from a TV commercial, so children's commercials benefit from being fast-paced (in fact, a normally paced commercial may bore them). If you are selling products to old age pensioners, DIY experts or 18-35-year-old females, find out about their interests, lifestyle and needs.

7 Summarize the benefits at the end of the commercial. Most viewers don't pick up much information. So keep the message clear and simple. At the end of the commercial, remind the viewer of the main benefit by summarizing it in a strapline or slogan. This should coincide with the pack super.

8 Leave the viewer with a picture of your pack. You want to sell your product, so finish with your logo. That is why the last frame must show the pack prominently. It can either be superimposed on to the existing scene, or the film could cut to a board. Add a 'call to action'. Tell the viewer what he should do. For example, 'Telephone 071-900 1000 for more information'.

METHODS OF APPROACH

Many commercials use a similar format. They start with a proposition, such as 'New White washing powder gets your clothes really clean'. This is followed by a second section, which adds proof or a demonstration. A final section summarizes the benefits.

In a variant on this theme, the commercial identifies a problem (plaque can cause gum disease). It then offers a solution (our improved toothpaste). Then it shows the result (healthy gums). Finally it ends with the pack shot.

No matter what format is chosen, most commercials fall

into distinct themes. Below we look at the main types of commercial.

Appetite appeal. Many commercials are for food products. Everyone eats food, and so the big food brands have a substantial advertising spend. It is essential to make food commercials appetizing. We should see the ingredients being mixed, the food sizzling on the grill, and (above all) people enjoying the taste. There is an old advertising saying, 'Sell the sizzle not the sausage', and this is especially true of food commercials. The commercial should make the viewer want to reach into the TV and grab some of the food.

Clown. This type of commercial features an idiot and an intelligent person. The intelligent person explains patiently why the clown should invest his money with a certain building society. The clown makes the lesson memorable and saves it from becoming pompous.

Cartoons suit TV admirably (if you have the right sort of product) because they are simple, lively, and dramatic. They can do things that human beings can't do (they can flood a carpet with tears, or leap ten feet in joy). Every brand is supposed to have a brand personality, and cartoons let you endow the brand with personality. They also let the product speak for itself, in the case of animated teabags or oranges.

Demonstration. Demonstration commercials are ideal for products that do things, such as lawnmowers. They can also illustrate the benefits of other types of products. A tyre commercial will show a car stopping fast, while a commercial for a magazine will take you through the main features. A toy commercial will show children demonstrating the features of a new toy by playing with it. Leisure parks show people enjoying the various rides and restaurants.

In a way, every commercial should be a demonstration, because it should show the product being used. People should eat your ice cream or drive your car.

Drama. Who are the silent investigators at a nuclear power plant? Answer: the general public who are allowed in every day. Will the executive successfully deliver his presentation, despite travelling a long distance? Answer: yes, because he has chosen a comfortable airline.

Endorsement. A famous personality tells the viewer why he chooses a particular brand of breakfast cereal. This method transfers to the brand the respect and loyalty that people have for the celebrity. If a famous sportsman says he always buys a certain fizzy drink, viewers believe it must have contributed to his performance and that it will boost their own.

Celebrities are unreliable. No sooner will your commercial have been made than the celebrity will go on trial for fraud or suffer a road traffic accident. Alternatively, his agent may decide to double the fees for the next commercial.

Exaggeration. One biscuit is so complete that it fills huge holes. Another bar is so light it lets you leap canyons. Exaggeration is a good means of making the commercial humorous and memorable. That is why it is often used for youth- and child-oriented products.

The expert. The Managing Director tells you his double-glazed windows are the best, while a doctor informs you that a new pill will relieve headaches. Some experts talk direct to the viewer, while others are shown giving advice to a housewife or a young couple. In recent years this theme has been turned on its head, with the man in the street getting his own back on the expert bank manager.

Fantasy. Children eat fishfingers on a galleon, a man parachutes to deliver chocolates to his girlfriend, and a woman travels to all parts of the world in her new car. Television is the ideal fantasy medium.

Humour. Humour allows the advertiser to put across a sales point in a light hearted way (see Clown above).

Life style. Aspirational commercials show beautiful girls and handsome men lazing on beaches drinking canned drinks. Alternatively, the commercial shows a wide variety of people enjoying the product, from window cleaners to executives. A variant is to show people with more than one life style (for example a car commercial that shows a couple equally at home in the town and country).

Mood. A product with no unique benefit can be promoted through a mood commercial. The mood might be rural, sophisticated, natural, introspective, light-hearted or elegant. Shampoo and perfume are two products for which an atmosphere is often created through photography alone. Some commercials manage to dispense with words almost completely.

Musical heritage. Commercials can use well-known records to reinforce images. They link the brand to earlier times when life seemed simpler. The commercials often relate to the viewer's childhood in the 1950s or 1960s.

News commercials. Once the mainstay of the commercial break, the 'new, improved' format is much less common now. This is partly because consumers are less ready to believe bland claims about 'new formula toothpaste with ZNX'. Perhaps we have moved into an era where continuous refinements in food formulae are less possible or even desirable. Non-food brands will continue to use this format.

Problem solution. A motorist is stranded at night, a shirt is heavily soiled, or a child can't tie her shoe-laces. These problems are resolved thanks to a motorists' organization, a soap powder or a breakfast cereal. This type of commercial usually contains an element of Drama (see above).

Proof. The corn is harvested at the right time, day or night – and the commercial proves this by showing combine harvesters crossing a field at night. The proof commercial takes a USP and dramatizes it.

Sex. A girl slowly devours a chocolate, gets undressed for a shower or lies on a beach. If you use the product (says the commercial), you too can be as sexy as the model. Research shows that people remember the sexy bits but forget the product that was being promoted. Use sex sparingly.

Slice of life. Two children argue at the meal table while devouring a new pizza. This tells us in an indirect way that the best way to feed lively children is to give them a particular brand of pizza.

Soap. For thirty seconds we eavesdrop on the relationships in a family or between lovers. A man borrows coffee from his female neighbour and stops to chat. We infer that clever up-market people drink a certain brand of coffee.

Talking head. One person, usually male, speaks direct to camera. It may lack dramatic impact, but when other commercials are full of song and dance, it stands out.

Two women in a kitchen. This commercial typically has two women comparing the whiteness of their washing. It is best to avoid clichés; but if you are unlucky enough to sell soap powder, you haven't much choice but to place your characters in a kitchen.

Many commercials mix different types of theme – for example fantasy and cartoon – so you can pick and mix your themes. You should also avoid using a worn-out theme. TV commercials go in waves. A commercial that shows businessmen as heroes will soon be followed by imitators. Finally, this treatment will be parodied by other commercials before the genre disappears for a while.

Mistakes to avoid
- Irritating, self-satisfied male character
- Simpering female character
- Smug message from the advertiser
- Raucous chorus
- Ranting, incessant talk
- Over-enthusiasm
- Dialogue that doesn't ring true
- Clichéd situations

Typical faults in TV commercials. Today's consumer is more

subtle, more sceptical and less naïve. Give her a commercial that flatters her, teases her or respects her.

WRITING POSTERS

Posters are cost-effective for many targets. Posters can reach 1,000 AB men at one-fifteenth of the cost of television. Posters also offer drama and impact. They are ideal for reaching mobile people who tend to be up-market, young and male.

Posters can target certain places, such as named supermarkets, motorway areas or London boroughs. They can also compliment television campaigns, by giving a more long-lasting message.

Posters are often used in 'teaser campaigns', especially for new product launches. They can announce that something important is about to happen, without revealing the product's name.

WHO USES POSTERS – AND WHO DOESN'T

Certain product categories make heavy use of posters. Car manufacturers like them because they show off the car on a grand scale and they reach car drivers who, by definition, are driving around. Posters are also used for products that are banned from television (such as cigarettes and spirits).

Posters are not suited to certain other product types. You can't show that food is tasty, or that an electric saw is easy to use. Nor, amid the roar of the traffic, can you imply that a perfume is calm and sophisticated. However, the absence of certain types of advertiser means a bigger opportunity for some brands. To prove the power of the medium, a poster contractor 'launched' a non-existent Australian perfume called 'Sheila', which achieved high awareness.

THINKING BIG

With posters, you have to think big and simple. Outdoor posters are seen by people who are travelling, whether in a car, a bus or on foot. People give each poster only a fleeting glance, so you have barely a few seconds to convey your message. That is why most posters have bold images.

There is another reason for thinking big. Many posters are pasted to hoardings high in the air or far from the pavement. People can't get close enough to read small copy, so there is no point in including detailed sales points in posters. If your advertisements need body copy to sell them, you should stay away from posters.

WHAT YOU CAN'T DO WITH POSTERS

Posters aren't good at getting people to act. They can't get passers-by to clip a coupon or post a cheque. Nor is there a phone handy. So posters aren't ideal for direct response advertisers, nor companies which want the reader to write for a brochure. That said, some charities use the drama of posters to convey their cause graphically.

Posters also miss people who stay indoors. People who stay at home aren't usually big spenders, so that isn't a problem for advertisers.

WHAT TO SAY – AND HOW TO SAY IT

A poster should have no more than six words, and three is better still. More than six words makes it difficult for the passer-by to understand the message, and visibility drops as the poster becomes more cluttered. The typeface must be bold and simple to ensure legibility.

The creative solution depends on the advertising brief. Car companies, for example, often want to contrast two benefits ('sporty but roomy', or 'fast but economical').

Imagine you want to promote a brand of olive oil. There are several possible creative solutions:

- It's the Italians' favourite
- It's been made since 1890
- It makes food taste delicious
- It's less calorific than other oils
- It's a healthy oil
- It's a pure, natural oil
- It's a genuine Italian product
- It's bought by young, cosmopolitan and fun-loving people
- It's used by a famous personality

The choice of proposition will have major impact on the creative treatment. A 'tasty' proposition will show people enjoying their food, while an 'Italian' proposition might show a typically Italian scene.

Research will identify which of these concepts is the most relevant. You then need a simple and attention-grabbing execution to communicate the concept.

COMPETING WITH OTHER POSTERS

To compete effectively with other advertisers, your poster must have as much impact as theirs. This normally means full-colour reproduction, which is expensive unless the cost is to be spread over a nationwide campaign. The exception would be dramatic black and white pictures (as with the charity mentioned earlier).

If your production budget is limited, you should consider other forms of outdoor posters. Bus backs, for example don't directly compete with full-colour 48 sheet posters, and are more suitable for smaller advertisers. They are often used by local garages, not (it has to be said) with much creative flair. But remember that no message is enhanced by being on the back of a dirty bus whose exhaust is pumping out black fumes – unless you are selling new exhausts.

HOW TO MAKE POSTERS WORK HARDER

Show a person: Human interest adds impact. For extra effect, the figure should be looking at the reader.

Make the message clear: Don't assume too much prior knowledge about the product, or familiarity with a TV campaign. The more obscure the poster, the fewer people will understand it.

Exploit the medium: Some posters have been designed to look torn, and others look as though they have been pasted up wrongly.

Don't use body copy – even on indoor posters: The poster is unlikely to be close to the customer. Therefore you should avoid using body copy. Make the poster bold and single-minded.

Stay in posters for a long period: The best poster sites are contracted to major companies for long periods. So new users often have to build up a portfolio over a long period of time.

Show the pack or brand name: It must be clearly visible. Unlike a press ad where the pack is often shown bottom right, it should be positioned centrally in a poster for better visibility.

Use bright colours: They give the poster more prominence. Muted colours and black and white posters blend into the urban environment and are less effective at selling.

Use humour: People like to be entertained. Witty posters have higher recall. People don't seek out advertising. You have to woo them and reward them for looking at your poster.

Make it local: You can localize your posters by adding dealers' names and addresses. This has to be done carefully if it isn't to look like a cheap afterthought.

MANUFACTURERS' POSTERS IN SHOPS

Manufacturers have found it increasingly difficult to get their posters into retail outlets, though the less sophisticated outlets are still willing to take them. Motor factors often have a mass of posters advertising spark plugs, car paint and fan belts. Many bookshops display publishers' posters.

A retailer will take a poster of products that can't easily be displayed. Outdoor play equipment is often sold from posters. You will need to take the size of the window or wall into account when designing the poster.

INDOOR POSTERS

Retailers can use posters to:

- Soften the harsh interior of a store, especially with photos.
- Announce services that are not visible (a bike retailer promoting its repair service).

- Announce special offers (garages promoting their trading stamps).
- Add value to the product by showing it at its best (butchers' posters showing choice cuts of meat in a meal).
- Enliven otherwise dull windows. This applies to banks, building societies, opticians and other service companies. These businesses don't have physical products to sell, and their interiors aren't very interesting. Service companies use posters to sell a financial service or to encourage people to have an eye test, but a secondary objective is to make the place look less bleak.

WALLCHARTS – THE HIGH-VALUE POSTER

Drug companies promote their products in health centres by sponsoring educational posters. This technique can be adapted for other markets. Posters can be distributed to schools, given as a free write-in, or be sent in return for coupons collected.

Any market which requires skill or knowledge is ideal for sponsored posters. Car maintenance, DIY, computing, child care, and health and fitness are typical examples.

The wallchart is ideal for providing long-term branding. It is also the exception to the usual rule that posters should be simple. A wallchart can be as detailed as the market will permit, and in some cases the more detail the better. A manufacturer of machine tools might use a poster to show all the available tools, and a computer software company might put instructions or tips on a wallchart.

A wallchart allows you to demonstrate expertise, even market leadership. By conveying objective information about your market, you make your business seem experienced and altruistic.

8 Other forms of writing: don't leave a stone unturned

Advertisements and newsletters may be the glamorous part of promotion, but there are many other important ways to communicate. In this chapter we look at:

- Proposals and estimates – used by many service companies as a promotional tool.
- Sales presenters – the traditional way of helping the sales force.
- Exhibition graphics – how to stop people in their tracks.
- Brand names – choosing a name that suits the brand.
- Retail windows – distinguishing your store from everyone else's.
- Labelling – a complex six-sided communications exercise.

WRITING A PROPOSAL

The proposal is often an old-fashioned, uninviting document. That is because they are often issued by an estimating or sales support department, whose priorities are accuracy and profitability, rather than the appearance of the document.

Companies have two bases on which to judge your proposal – the price and everything else. It is in your interest to focus attention on the non-price elements. So it is vital that your proposal sells your services in the most attractive way.

Why companies buy a proposal
Price
Reputation

Integrity
Service
Speed of delivery
Human factors (personal chemistry)
Professionalism
Experience
Understanding the client's needs
Ability to solve problems

Do all these factors stand out in your proposals?

CONTENTS OF AN ESTIMATE OR PROPOSAL

There are four elements to a proposal: the covering letter, the estimate or quotation, company or product information, and the folder to carry all this information.

For simple quotations, all the information will be included in a letter, while more complex quotations will need to be in a separate document.

The *letter* needs to be friendly: it should show that you want the customer's business. Unless the quotation has a low sales value, the covering letter should be properly personalized. It is not enough to send a standard letter. Personalization is even more important if the quotation includes an element of service (for example, maintenance). The recipient will judge your future service by the effort you put into his quotation.

Company or product information has been discussed under 'Dynamic sales literature' (see page 102). Many service companies neglect to include a brochure with their proposals. For example, a car-leasing company should include a manufacturer's brochure illustrating the vehicles. The same applies to service companies who supply mobile phones or computers.

If your *proposal* is a long one, you should provide a brief management summary. This should be short enough to be read in a few minutes, but long enough to do justice to your effort.

Some companies present a bound document. Others, who have several different pieces of paper, place all the information inside a *folder*. Whichever method you adopt, the material should be attractively designed and, if the economics justify it, be printed in full colour. Short-run colour reproduction is much simpler and cheaper than it used to be.

A proposal should start selling from the title. Don't use a bland title like:

Proposals for a new llama shed
for Puddlemarsh Zoo

It will be better to state the advantages of your work:

Comfortable new living accommodation
for llamas at Puddlemarsh Zoo
offering improved visitor access
and leading to increased revenues

Decide what you are selling and put that in the title. Sign companies aren't selling signs, they're selling communication, flexibility and interior design.

The proposal document will need to include the following items, many parts of which can come from standard files on your word processor.

Contents of a proposal
Analysis of the brief
Objectives
Action taken
Review of the current situation
Method/Strategy/Plan/Action
Benefits
Previous experience
Costs
Personnel
Timing

Analysis of the brief
A written brief tells you two things: you are dealing with a professional organization, and at least one other company is competing for the work.

It is worth looking at the brief in some detail. Do you agree with the brief in all points? If not, why do you disagree? Perhaps you have recently conducted some research that shows a better way to tackle the task? Or maybe your experience tells you that the project must have a different starting point? There are several reasons for evaluating a brief:

1   You may want to change the brief for the client's benefit. In other words, you might have a more cost-effective way of proceeding.
2   You may want to move the goalposts, to prevent another competitor from succeeding. This is a gamble, because the client may prefer the goalposts where they were.
3   You may want to concentrate on certain parts of the brief if it is too broad.
4   Parts of the brief may conflict or be mutually incompatible.

Objectives: State the objectives clearly. This prevents misunderstanding later in the presentation when the client says 'But I thought we were trying to ...

Action taken: What action did you take in response to the client's brief? Who in the client company was interviewed – list the individuals, together with their titles and geographic locations. Include a list of documents studied, and authorities consulted.

Review of the situation: This section could analyse the market, or review the client's business. It sums up the lessons that have been learnt from the investigation, and states where the problem lies or the way it should be approached.

Method: This section will be structured according to the project. The solution might be described by time, by geography or department, or by type of equipment.
What fresh thinking can you bring to the project? This is the one area where you can score over the competition, and

demonstrate to the client that you have soundly understood his problem.

In a presentation, there is a tendency to keep this section as late as possible – to keep the client expectant, and to build a climax. In the written document, the section needs to go in its logical place, which will be somewhere in the middle, after the introduction and analysis, but before the costing and the staff biographies.

The benefits: What benefits will accrue to the buyer if he puts the project in your hands? Do you have a centralized buying department that reduces costs by 20 per cent? Do you have an information service that produces a monthly industry report? Do you have a range of ancillary services that the client can use if necessary? Is the project manager on call around the clock?

Previous experience: What similar work have you carried out recently? What were the similarities and the differences? What did the company learn during the course of the work?

Costs: You have hopefully worked up the client's enthusiasm to a point where the price is not so important. You should have demonstrated that, even if you aren't the cheapest company, you are the best.

Personnel: Who will handle the project? What experience do they have? Who have they worked for before? Who will manage the team? And will the team that does the work be the same as the one that is presenting the proposals?

Timing: When will you start, and when will the project be completed? For some firms this is crucial (in shop-fitting, for example, where closure or disruption means lost income).

Don't feel constrained by these headings – add your own as appropriate. You could for example, add a checklist for the client to see if your competitors have the same skills.

THE SALES PRESENTER

Sales presenters (or sales promoters as they are sometimes known) usually consist of single sheets inserted into a display book which has transparent A4 pockets. This lets the presentation remain flexible. The representative can arrange the contents according to the needs of the customer, and old sheets can be removed without having to reprint the whole presenter.

A sales presenter is a valuable tool. It ensures that all the sales points are covered, and that they are presented professionally, accurately and in the right order. It also boosts the customer's understanding, because he both hears and sees the sales message.

HOW A SALES PRESENTER IS USED

Consider the circumstances of the rep's visit. The buyer is busy, and seeing a rep isn't one of his favourite jobs. The meeting takes place under difficult surroundings – the phone rings and visitors interrupt. The meeting may even take place on the sales floor, with the buyer strolling about. This means that the presenter has to be as simple as possible. The information must flow logically from one topic to the next, and the words must be relevant to the buyer.

FIVE WAYS TO MAKE A PRESENTER MORE SUCCESSFUL

1 **Decide your objective** in producing a presenter. This will improve its clarity. If your objective is to launch a new promotion, the presenter will look very different from one which is aiming to increase your distribution.

2 **Use simple charts and diagrams** to illustrate sales growth, market share or customer attitudes.

3 **Use colour for effect.** Print colour pictures of new products, the head office, the customer's logo, or anything else that will brighten the page. Today's colour copiers and desktop publishing systems have substantially reduced the price of short-run colour reproduction.

4 **Only cover one set of sales points on each sheet.** This will make the page easier to understand, and will prevent it from becoming cluttered.

5 **Reduce the words to a minimum,** using bullet points where required.

DRAFTING AN OUTLINE

A sales presenter should not be simply a collection of statistics or pictures of products. Before writing a sales presenter, first produce an outline. This will provide a framework for the words and pictures.

The outline could look like this:

Page 1   Market size

Page 2   Consumer profile

Page 3   Bloggs market share

Page 4   Current Bloggs range

Page 5   Sales of Bloggs products in this outlet over the last twelve months

Page 6   New product 1, photo and name

Page 7   Sales points of new product 1

Page 8   New product 2, photo and name

Page 9   Sales points for product 2

Page 10   Launch promotion – advertising

Page 11   Launch promotion – dealer incentives

Page 12   Launch promotion – consumer sales promotion

Page 13   Summary page

Page 14   Order form

Already we have fourteen sheets, and there is a danger of over-burdening the customer with facts and figures.

WRITING THE SALES PRESENTER

You might start with a title page:

The Suet Market
The rich one!

Some companies leave room for the sales rep to personalize the front page for each customer, as in:

Happy Cow Suet
and
_____

The first page could present key facts about the market and the product:
- £8 million worth of suet sales every year
- Four million housewives buy suet
- Used in many ways: mince pies, as a tasty snack
- Only natural ingredients
- Long established
- Cheaper than butter

At this point the presenter might focus on the company's brand:

Happy Cow Suet brand
- The market leader
- Premium price
- Smooth texture
- In blind tests, three out of ten housewives couldn't tell Fat Cow suet from butter

Note how few words there are. Swathes of text would look off-putting for the buyer, and might tempt him to end the interview.

THEMES FOR SALES PRESENTERS
It is useful to decide a theme for the sales presenter. Put this theme at the bottom of each page, as a way of holding the presentation together. However, extra words can distract the buyer's attention, so use this device with caution.

Here are some themes. Each promotes a particular sales point. For example, the first is for a new entrant into the market, while the second is defending market share with new products.

- The new force in the market
- Innovation from the market leader
- Better products, more profits
- Customer-driven success
- Clean up in our spring campaign
- Quality products mean bigger profits

At the end of the presentation, you should have a summary, which acts as a résumé of all the points covered.

Alternatively, you could insert an order form. This will concentrate the rep's mind on the job in hand – to win sales. After all, the presenter's prime function is not to entertain the customer but to win more orders.

Check list
Points to include in a sales presenter:

Range
Colours
Price, retail/wholesale margin
Promotion (to the trade, to the consumer)
Sales aids (literature, posters, point of sales material)
The consumer (who buys?)
The company – scale, market share, R&D facilities
Services – technical back-up
Quality, reliability
New products (size, shape, functions, benefits, the gap in the market)
Recommended shelf layout
Order details (minimum order size)
Delivery times
Tailor-made products or promotions
Case histories, previous successes
Order form

WRITING FOR EXHIBITIONS

We have all seen footsore visitors walking past rows of stands that offer similar merchandise. Wary of being accosted by sales reps, the visitor eyes each stand as he passes, checking that he isn't missing anything important.

This means that the words for exhibition stands have to work like posters. They must attract the attention of people who are scurrying past, and they compete for attention with countless other messages.

Exhibition words must be simple and bold. They should attract the attention and create desire. You should reduce the message to its simplest element, and sell the benefits of the product. It isn't enough to put up the names of your products, nor simply to rely on your company name. You must decide why people buy your product. Why do they buy it in preference to the product being offered in the stand opposite?

The visitor must be told *why* the product is superior, if he is to stop. The exhibition graphics must communicate fully with the visitor who stops at the stand when all the salesmen are busy. The buyer may not be ready to talk to a salesman. Perhaps he wants to decide for himself whether the product is suitable for his needs?

All this emphasizes the importance of good selling text on the exhibition stand. Decide on the sales points you want to convey. You will need to make the most of the available space, but leave enough blank wall to prevent the text from looking cramped and illegible. Remember to add visual information to provide complete information for the visitor.

Check list for exhibition graphics
Is the information bold?
Can it be quickly and easily understood?
Does it explain what the company does?
Does it contain benefits?
Is it legible from the aisle?
Is it visible above the exhibits and literature displays?
Will it make someone want to visit the stand?

CREATING BRAND-NAMES

Creating brand-names is a thankless task; but unless you hand the job over to a professional brand-name company or an advertising agency, you will probably have to do it yourself.

It is important to agree a brief (see check list below), and to limit the number of people involved. Otherwise you will never get agreement – there will always be one or two people who don't like the proposed name. If too many people are involved, the chosen name will be the one which arouses least discussion. It will be the lowest common denominator, a name which will be greeted with equal apathy in the market-place.

A new name is likely to have between one and three syllables. More than that will make it difficult to remember and cumbersome to say.

Avoid the obvious names. Companies like certain names which always occur in a wide range of products. Fiesta, for example, is applied to everything from paper towels to motor-cars. Beware of words that sound old-fashioned, such as those that start with Hi-, or Nu-.

You can take names from places, from people, or from other objects. Music, the sea, ancient gods, and animals are often chosen. Brand-names are sometimes taken from popular songs, which gives the brand its own ready-made jingle and a set of positive associations. A scheme to let first-time buyers buy their home without saving up was called 'Walk Right In', which suggested the ease of buying the house.

If you find the best names have been taken, you could use a Christian name. A plastic support for compact discs was named Max and given human attributes ('Put Max in your CD player ... ')

Masculine products are often given aggressive names (Charger, Lynx), while feminine products are usually softer. There are exceptions, however, with perfumes being given names like Poison.

Brand-names can have a double meaning. A new birthing bed to help women deliver was called Birthright. This played on the idea of women giving birth the right way, and the baby's right to an easy birth.

Products which are to be sold in foreign countries are often given Italianate names (Concerto, Nova) which sound universal.

Some names are formed from analogies; for example, a

twin-bladed razor called Slalom. The analogy doesn't have to be exact. You may simply want to convey an image or an emotion. Remember, too, that once the brand-name is established it takes on its own characteristics, which are different from the original name. The word 'Cargo' summons up a different set of images for a lorry driver than it does for a seaman.

New products are often named after the job they do – which can lead to them becoming a generic name (as with Sellotape).

Some names are relatively easy to devise. A new brand of bread would need to sound fresh, wholesome, natural, and of the country. We might end up with words like Woodland, Furrow or Sunrise. A new pension plan might need to imply wealth, security and comfort. It might be called Foresight, Stronghold or Exchequer.

Before you invest large sums of money in the new name, check that it isn't the property of another company or a registered trade mark. Companies are highly protective of their names. An organization for home-based workers had to change its name from Homebase when Sainsbury's DIY chain of the same name objected, despite the fact that the club had no interest in DIY or retailing.

Most of the good words are already in use. If you come across the perfect name, it is almost certain to have been taken. New brands now have to accept names that are not closely related to the product. This challenge often leads to more creative brand-names.

CHECK LIST FOR A NEW BRAND-NAME
Values: What values should the brand encompass?
Target consumer: Is the consumer male or female, ABC1 or C2DE? Urban, suburban, or rural? Does he buy other products from the company?
Consumer characteristics: What other characteristics does he have? Under what circumstances is the product used – in the home, in a pub, with friends, at an office, in a lunch break?
Tone of voice: Should it be cosy and friendly, or sharp and uncompromising.

Location: Will the product be sold abroad? If so, the name will have to sound right to foreign ears, and be available.

TECHNIQUES FOR CHOOSING A NAME
Brainstorming. Brainstorming involves a group of four to ten people who suggest names. All the names are written down, with none being criticized. A target of 50-100 names could be set. Synectics is like brainstorming, except that it is more directed. The leader tells the group about the product, and they suggest names. The leader provides feedback to the group by pointing out the strengths and weaknesses of the suggestions.

Creating sounds. For a food product, you might want a word with lots of 'mmm', to conjure up satisfaction and filling. A new tennis racket might need a lot of 's' sounds to convey the idea of a ball hissing through the air at great speed.

Joined words. Some companies solve the problem by joining two words together. Imagine, for example, you had to create a new name for an organic compost. You could take a number of related words:

> Green, fertilizer, compost, rural, home, meadow, sweet, rich, garden, grow ...

You can then join parts of these words together in an infinite number of variations. The name could be anything from 'Greenmead' to 'GardenRich'.

The thesaurus. Don't neglect the thesaurus. It is a fertile source of words, and if you want a simple name, it will be in the thesaurus somewhere. A few hours spent looking at different sections can produce good names.

RETAIL WINDOWS

As stores get larger, their windows become increasingly less important. For out-of-town stores and city-centre grocery superstores, the windows are less likely to attract shoppers, and security has become a bigger consideration. As a result, some stores are almost totally lacking in windows.

Some retailers want to give the consumer a clear view into the shop. Their windows are empty of displays or posters.

At the other extreme, many high street shops make extensive use of their windows for display. For jewellers and estate agents, much of their selling is conducted in the window – with the consumer choosing a house or necklace while standing outside the store.

Many high-street stores which use window displays let their products do the selling. Fashion or leisure stores usually display their products without using words. Other retailers need to tell the consumer about products or services which can't be seen from the windows. A repair service or a credit plan are two examples. Sale posters are essential to spread the word about reduced prices.

Outlets with the greatest need for window display are service companies. Banks, building societies and opticians lack the attractions of branded merchandise, so they need to enliven their windows with attractive messages. Some give them over to local charities, while others promote their latest financial plan or savings account.

The more complicated the product, the greater the need to communicate it effectively. Instant print shops, for example, need to communicate their fax, binding and colour copying service. Such businesses often use plastic lettering which adheres to the window. These messages can be in the form of bullet points.

Information that needs words
Few retailers use words properly to provide information to potential purchasers. Consider the messages that a retailer might want to deliver, and which can only be communicated with words:

Quality (whether properly made, using quality fabrics, or reliable method of construction)
Guarantees
Environmentally friendly
Exclusive distribution rights

Cleanliness, pleasant staff
Mothers' room, clean toilets

LABELLING

Many companies see the pack as primarily a visual exercise, while their design agencies strive for maximum clarity and attractiveness. For them, the design of the product name, the shape of the pack and the method of dispensing are the key criteria.

But as the consumer becomes more aware – of ingredients, production techniques, the environment and over-packaging – the words become more important. Today the consumer wants information about the products she buys, and labels are becoming more detailed.

Apart from the base, the pack has five sides. Because products are displayed or stocked in different ways, the consumer may initially see any one of these sides. Each one must present a recognizable and uniform image that will act as a flag to the consumer.

The pack also needs to show essential information (the brand name, the description of what it does, and the pack size) on several sides.

When it comes to household products, the labelling needs to be highly visible. Some women with imperfect eyesight are reluctant to wear glasses when out shopping, and so they tend to choose products that stand out on the shelf.

Labels must be easily understood. What, for example is the housewife to make of this mysterious chart on a pack of washing powder?

	Percentage Range	Ingredients
Contains amongst other ingredients	30% and more	Anionic surfactants

It is important to avoid spurious 'green' claims. The consumer's knowledge is rapidly growing and, fed by the media, she is learning to distrust misleading claims.

The pack copy should communicate:

- The brand name and brand values.
- Statutory information (country of origin and ingredient list).
- Other practical information about pack weight or flavour.
- Recommendations about how the product should be used.
- Hints or tips about making the product last longer or work more efficiently.
- Consumerist information about the environment, including recommendations for disposal of the pack.
- The company name, and how to return the product if faulty.
- A competitive advantage (through design or copy), giving the purchaser a reason to buy this product rather than any other.

Some of the information can be in the form of symbols (for example the bar code, recycling mark, British Standard or EC standard weight).

Labelling information
Brand name
Descriptor (what the product does)
Contents
Weight
Price
Company name
Company address
Country of origin
Materials used in construction
Washing instructions
Assembly instructions
Instructions for use
Application (what it is suitable for)
Size
Colour
Quantity of units in the pack
'Use by' date

Environmental information
Disposal instructions
Safety notice – for poisons, or flammable products
Quality – a statement describing the quality of manufacture or ingredients
Certification marks (BSI kitemark)
Opening instructions (for tamper-evident or childproof closures)
Storage instructions
Promotional offers (extra volume or free gift)
Bar code
Manufacturers' serial code
Date of manufacture
Corporate information: date of company's establishment
What to do if the product doesn't work. How to complain
Promotional copy: reasons to choose this brand rather than any other
Instructions to retailer for stock rotation (outer container)
Instructions to distributor for stacking and transportation (outer container)

Index